Message from the BBG Chairman

On behalf of the Broadcasting Board of Governors, I am pleased to present the BBG's Performance and Accountability Report (PAR) for Fiscal Year (FY) 2014. This report includes the results of this year's audit of the Agency's financial statements; measures our performance against our FY 2014 objectives; highlights the accomplishments of the past year; and identifies the challenges that lie ahead.

The mission of the BBG is to inform, engage, and connect people around the world in support of freedom and democracy. The BBG broadcast services include two federal entities: the Voice of America (VOA) and the Office of Cuba Broadcasting (OCB); and three BBG-sponsored grantees: Radio Free Europe/Radio Liberty (RFE/RL), Radio Free Asia (RFA), and the Middle East Broadcasting Networks (MBN).

BBG networks are news leaders, uncovering stories left untold in environments that lack press freedom. In 2014, BBG networks were the first international broadcasters live streaming the events from the Maidan in Ukraine, have led coverage on the rise of Islamic State of Iraq and the Levant, and are currently reporting from the frontlines of the Ebola crisis.

Freedom and access to news and information is a right that the BBG holds in the highest regards. By exemplifying free media and free expression, the BBG helps foster and sustain free and democratic societies. The BBG networks pursue this mission through their own media via television, radio, Internet, social and mobile platforms, but also by working closely with media partners on the ground that bring our content into local markets, establishing valuable connections to critical institutions that influence civil society and democratic principles.

Today, the BBG networks are reaching a record worldwide audience of 215 million people in 61 languages. Recognizing that having impact requires more than just reaching large audiences, the BBG began implementation of its new impact model. This model outlines how BBG networks can be influential among audience members, media institutions, and governments in the short, medium, and long term and takes into account quantitative, qualitative, and anecdotal data.

BBG networks also help support specific U.S. foreign policy objectives. The BBG is increasingly focused on reaching large audiences in strategically important countries. For example, countering Russian propaganda in Ukraine with fact-based, objective journalism; providing a counter narrative to extremist propaganda in Syria, Iraq, East Africa, and Nigeria; combatting censorship in China by tapping into internal viral networks with coverage of taboo subjects including high-level government corruption and ethnic unrest; and sharing lifesaving health information with audiences in the Ebola-affected regions of West Africa.

In 2014, two driving forces of change have increased the agility of our networks: increased collaboration and the focus on strategic audiences. As the Ukraine Maidan protests turned violent, VOA expanded its reporting from Washington, D.C. to ensure that Ukrainian audiences knew that the United States supported their democratic goals. RFE/RL surged its reporting resources in Crimea and Eastern Ukraine to uncover the stories of Russian influence, including some of the first pictures of Russian equipment crossing the Ukrainian border. VOA and RFE/RL jointly created "Current Time," a new 30-minute television news program that is being carried on national channels in the Baltics, Ukraine, and Moldova as a foundation to a global response strategy to Russian propaganda.

This cooperation is also a conscious strategy of the Board in the current environment of increased competition and decreasing budgets. The BBG is undertaking active efforts to harmonize broadcasts, share resources, and incorporate new technologies to reach audiences. In Eurasia, the Balkans, and Iran, the Board is implementing new models that mandate close collaboration, differentiated content strategies and shared distribution. In FY 2015, that effort will be extended to Afghanistan, Pakistan, Southeast Asia, and Iraq.

In FY 2014, the BBG continued to fight for the free flow of information around the world. BBG Internet anti-censorship efforts included countering Internet censorship in 13 countries; supporting 21 BBG language services; and distributing circumvention tools, such as a mobile application for Android devices that incorporates a social news reader, a social reporter to accept user-generated content, and real-time chat functionality targeted at users in Iran.

The financial and performance data presented in this report are fundamentally complete and reliable. I am pleased that the independent auditors have given our financial statements an unqualified opinion for the tenth year. I recognize that there are a number of significant items identified by the external audit that will require our continued attention, diligence, and improvement. We are committed to addressing these items and meeting these challenges.

I am proud to report the achievements of the Broadcasting Board of Governors during FY 2014. We strive to wisely and effectively use the resources entrusted to us by the Administration, Congress, and the public to further our mission.

Jeffrey Shell
Chairman
November 17, 2014

BBG FY 2014 PERFORMANCE AND ACCOUNTABILITY REPORT:

Table of Contents

Introduction **5**

Section 1: Management's Discussion and Analysis **7**

Organizational Structure and Mission 8

FY 2014 Performance Goals and Objectives 10

Performance Highlights 11

Ongoing Challenges 14

Financial Highlights 19

Management Assurances 20

Limitations on Financial Statements 24

Section 2: Performance Information **25**

FY 2014 Goals, Objectives, and Results 26

Verification and Validation of Performance Measures 60

FY 2014 Performance Objectives and Outcomes 61

Summary of FY 2014 Performance Accomplishments 64

Use of Performance Data to Promote Improved Outcomes 74

Independent Program Evaluations 76

Section 3: Financial Information **81**

Letter from the Chief Financial Officer 82

Independent Auditor's Report 84

Response to the Audit 100

Balance Sheet 101

Statement of Net Cost 102

Statement of Changes in Net Position 103

Statement of Budgetary Resources 104

Notes to Principal Financial Statements 106

Required Supplementary Information 126

Section 4: Other Information **127**

Inspector General's Statement on FY 2014
Management and Performance Challenges 128

Agency Response to the Management and Performance Challenges 131

Summary of Financial Statement Audit and Management Assurances 134

Reporting on Improper Payments Information Act 136

Introduction

PURPOSE OF THE PERFORMANCE AND ACCOUNTABILITY REPORT

This FY 2014 Performance and Accountability Report (PAR) is the Broadcasting Board of Governors' (BBG) eleventh report providing performance and financial information. This integrated presentation of the Agency's program performance, financial accountability, and managerial effectiveness is intended to assist Congress, the President, and the public in assessing the BBG's performance relative to its mission and stewardship of the resources entrusted to it.

This report satisfies the reporting requirements of the following legislation:

- Federal Managers' Financial Integrity Act of 1982 (FMFIA)

- Government Performance and Results Act of 1993 (GPRA)

- Government Management Reform Act of 1994 (GMRA)

- Reports Consolidation Act of 2000

- Accountability of Tax Dollars Act of 2002

- Improper Payments Information Act of 2002

- Improper Payments Elimination and Recovery Act of 2010

- Improper Payments Elimination and Recovery Improvement Act of 2012

- Government Performance and Results Modernization Act of 2010 (GPRAMA)

STRUCTURE OF THE PERFORMANCE AND ACCOUNTABILITY REPORT

The report includes the following sections:

Management's Discussion and Analysis (MD&A)

The MD&A is an overview of the BBG, its organizational structure, and mission. It includes a summary of the Agency's program highlights and accomplishments for FY 2014 and the BBG's management and performance challenges. The MD&A also includes the results of the Agency's FY 2014 FMFIA internal control review and a section on management assurances.

Performance Information

The performance section presents annual program performance information as required by GPRA and GPRAMA and describes the Agency's progress in meeting its operational strategic goals. A summary of the FY 2014 performance objectives is presented, as well as information about the outcome of specific performance indicator targets and a summary explanation of the verification and validation of performance measures used in the report.

Financial Information

The financial section contains BBG's financial statements for the federal entities and the related Independent Auditor's Report. In this section, the BBG has prepared and presented all four statements as required by the Office of Management and Budget (OMB) Circular A-136, Financial Reporting Requirements.

Other Information

The other information section contains the Inspector General's statement on management and performance challenges along with the BBG's response. It also contains a summary of financial statement, audit, and management assurances and improper payments information.

Section 1:
Management's Discussion and Analysis

Organizational Structure and Mission 8

FY 2014 Performance Goals and Objectives 10

Performance Highlights 11

Ongoing Challenges 14

Financial Highlights 19

Management Assurances 20

Limitations on Financial Statements 24

Organizational Structure and Mission

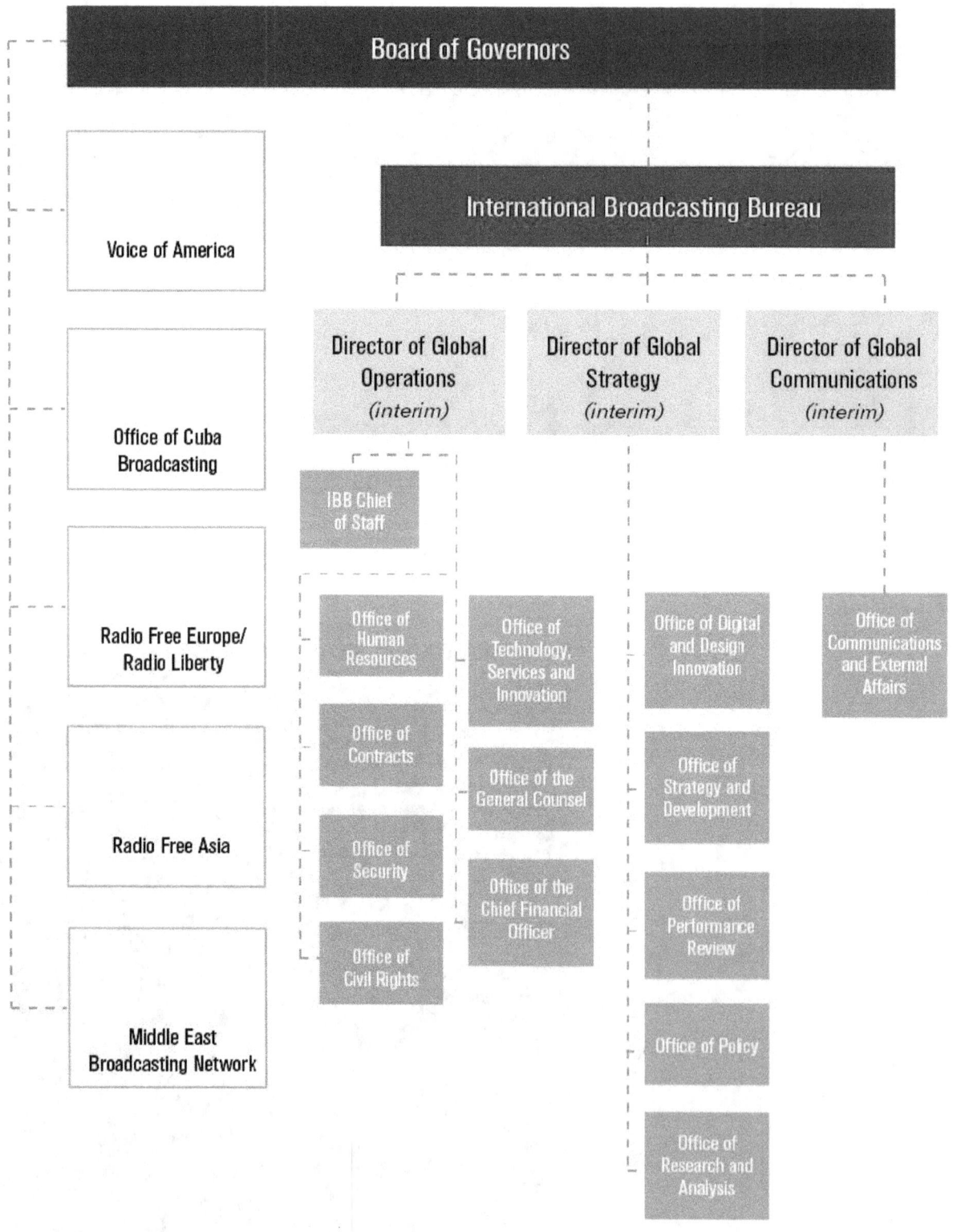

BBG ORGANIZATION

The Broadcasting Board of Governors (BBG) became an independent federal entity on October 1, 1999, as a result of the 1998 Foreign Affairs Reform and Restructuring Act (Public Law 105-22). The BBG administers civilian international media funded by the U.S. Government in accordance with the U.S. International Broadcasting Act of 1994, as amended. As set forth in the enabling legislation, a bi-partisan, presidentially appointed board serves as head of the Agency. BBG is the name of both the Agency and the Board that governs the Agency. The Board sets the priorities and overall strategic direction of U.S. international media, allocates resources, manages relationships with the other executive branch agencies and Congress, reviews and evaluates the effectiveness of the broadcast language services, and safeguards journalistic integrity. This last function is of key importance to the Board, which has a vital role as a "firewall" between BBG journalists and those who would seek to influence news coverage.

The BBG networks include the Voice of America (VOA), the Office of Cuba Broadcasting (OCB), Radio Free Europe/Radio Liberty (RFE/RL), Radio Free Asia (RFA), and the Middle East Broadcasting Networks (MBN), as well as management and support offices in the International Broadcasting Bureau (IBB).

VOA, OCB, RFE/RL, RFA, and MBN, while under the direction of the BBG, have varied legal and organizational frameworks. VOA and OCB are part of the federal government. RFE/RL, RFA, and MBN are surrogate broadcasters that receive funding from the federal government but are organized and managed as private non-profit corporations.

BBG MISSION

To inform, engage, and connect people around the world in support of freedom and democracy.

The Broadcasting Board of Governors (BBG) informs, engages, and connects people around the world in support of freedom and democracy through its international media programs. The BBG reaches a worldwide audience of 215 million via radio, television, and the Internet. All BBG broadcast services adhere to the standards and principles of the International Broadcasting Act of 1994, as amended, and support the BBG mission.

FY 2014 Goals and Objectives

In the Strategic Plan covering FY 2014-2018, the BBG has set two strategic goals:

- **Expand freedom of information and expression**
- **Communicate America's democratic experience**

In support of these goals, the Strategic Plan sets out six Strategic Objectives and three Management Objectives:

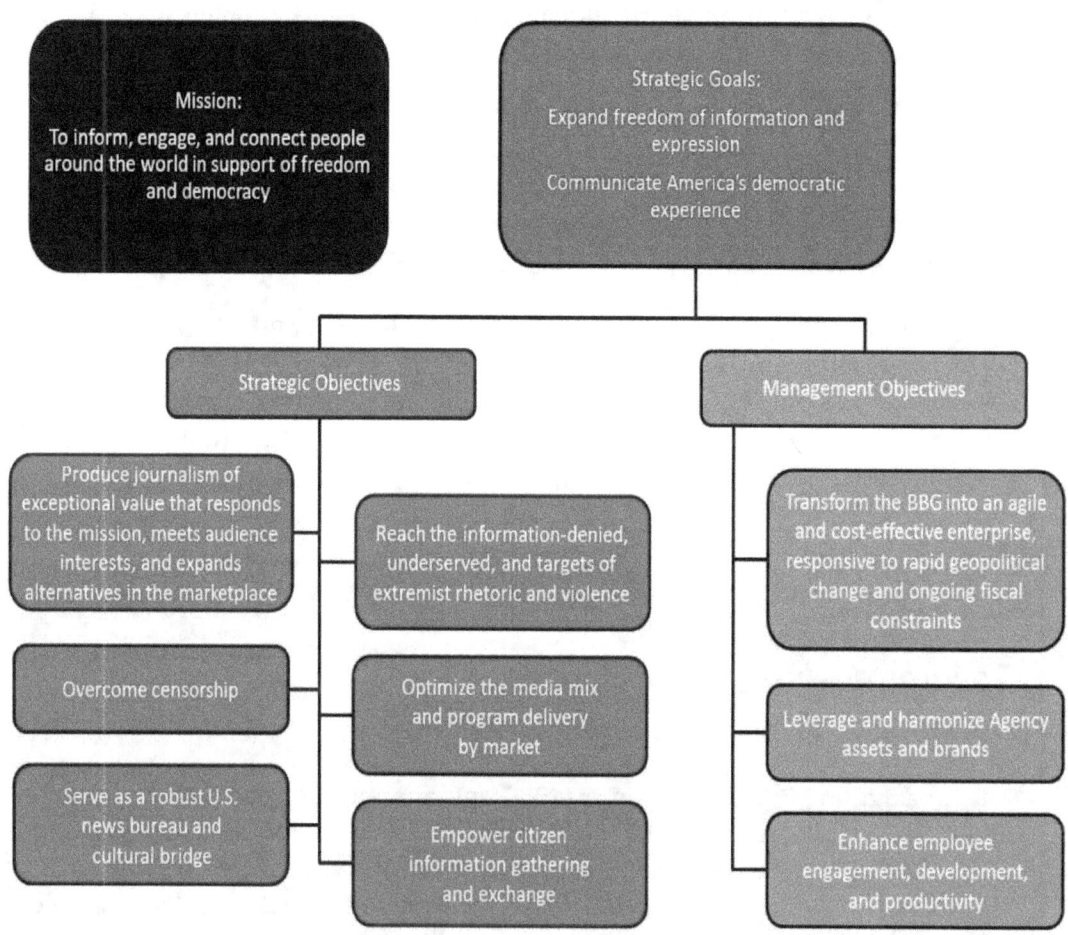

The Agency set performance goals supporting each of the Strategic and Management Objectives. Highlights of BBG's performance in FY 2014 are presented on the following pages. Full performance results are presented in Section Two.

Performance Highlights

Over the past year, the BBG has effectively distributed breaking news, in-depth reporting and reasoned analysis on traditional and new media platforms, illustrating that international media is the most effective U.S. tool to provide accurate news and information and relevant discussions to those who do not receive this from their own media.

The broadcasts of the BBG entities reach a worldwide audience of 215 million in 61 languages.

Global
English
Learning English

Eastern/ Central Europe
Albanian
Bosnian
Croatian
Macedonian
Montenegrin
Romanian
Serbian

Eurasian
Armenian
Avar
Azerbaijani
Bashkir
Belarusian
Chechen
Circassian
Crimean Tatar
Georgian
Russian
Tatar
Ukrainian

Central Asia
Kazakh
Kyrgyz
Tajik
Turkmen
Uzbek

East Asia
Burmese
Cantonese
Indonesian
Khmer
Korean
Lao
Mandarin
Thai
Tibetan
Uyghur
Vietnamese

South Asia
Bangla
Dari
Pashto
Persian
Urdu

Latin America
Creole
Spanish

Africa
Afan Oromo
Amharic
Bambara
French-to-Africa
Hausa
Kinyarwanda
Kirundi
Ndebele
Portuguese-to-Africa
Sango
Shona
Somali
Songhai
Swahili
Tigrigna

Middle East/ North Africa
Arabic
Kurdish
Turkish

Voice of America (VOA)
Radio Free Europe/Radio Liberty (RFE/RL)
Radio Free Asia (RFA)
Office of Cuba Broadcasting (OCB)
Middle East Broadcasting Network (MBN)

61 languages

Key accomplishments in FY 2014 include:

- MBN provided in-depth coverage of the Syria civil war and refugee crisis, sectarian violence in Iraq, and elections in Iraq, Egypt, Tunisia, and Algeria.

- VOA and RFE/RL ramped up Ukrainian coverage and added new programs in response to events in the region. They jointly reach one in five adults in Ukraine weekly.

- RFA and VOA provided news and information on the protests in Hong Kong for audiences in mainland China, despite media blackouts, with a multi-platform strategy.

- VOA expanded programming across the critical Sahel region of Africa, with new programs and broadcasts for Nigeria, Central African Republic, South Sudan, and Mali.

- OCB launched *Reporta Cuba*, a network of citizen reporters who use new media tools to disseminate information and report their experiences, without censorship.

Top: In March 2014, VOA & Radio Sawa launched a new FM station in N'Djamena, Chad.

Bottom:

Alhurra correspondent provides coverage of the Egyptian elections.

VOA reporters cover a protest in Ukraine.

STRATEGIC OBJECTIVE 1:

Produce journalism of exceptional value that responds to the mission, meets audience interests, and expands alternatives in the marketplace

Performance Goal 1: Reach significant audiences

A key measure of BBG's success is its weekly audience. These charts present weekly audience for BBG broadcasters from FY 2010 to FY 2014, along with the targets set by the Agency.

Impact cannot be reduced to a single quantitative factor. The BBG has developed new impact model, supported by a robust set of new performance indicators to gauge success. Many of these indicators have been incorporated into other performance goals.

Further discussion of these figures and results for the other performance goals and indicators are presented in Section Two: Performance Information.

* National estimates of audience reach for OCB in Cuba are not available. For more information, please see page 30.

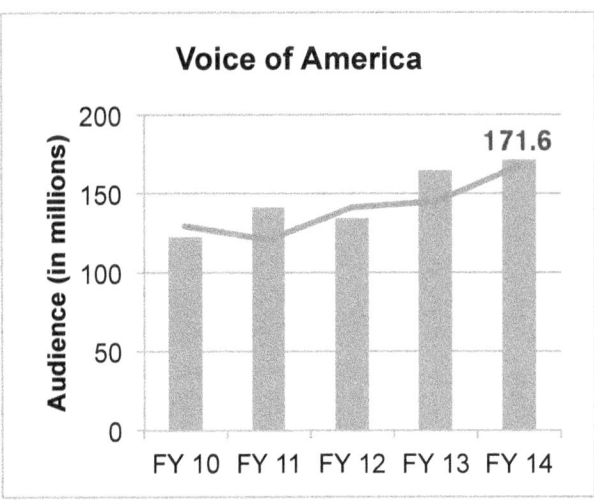

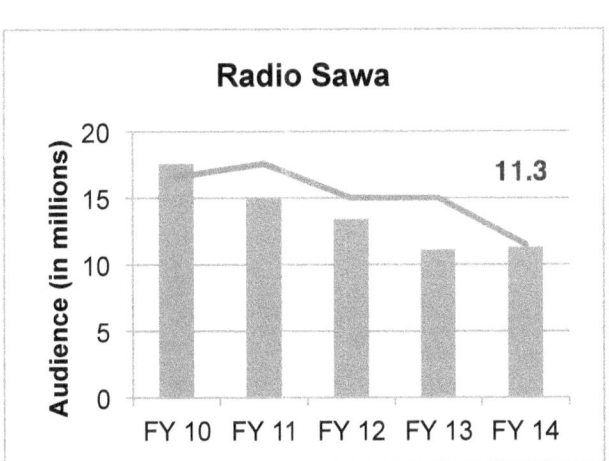

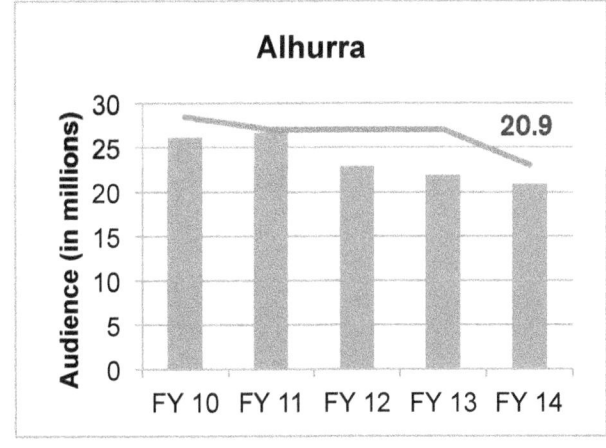

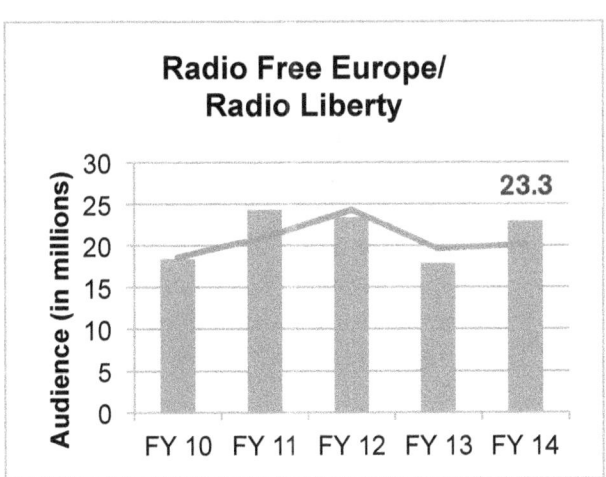

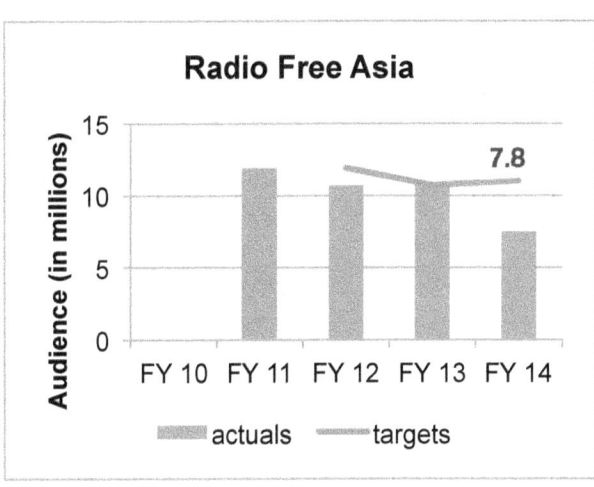

Ongoing Challenges

MEDIA ENVIRONMENT

Two major factors shape the global political and security context for BBG operations: extreme volatility in global affairs and the need to sustain a global information posture. Extremist rhetoric and incitement to violence directly threaten U.S. national security interests in Iraq, Syria, Afghanistan, the FATA, the Maghreb, the Sahel, Yemen, Somalia, and elsewhere, while the surprisingly adroit adaptation of digital and social media by hostile non-state actors around the world, including the Islamic State, Boko Haram, Al Qaeda, and others, threatens core U.S. values of freedom and democracy and respect for human rights as they seek to instill fear and intimidation among local populations. The BBG brands' credible, factual, and locally relevant journalism counters these lies and half-truths and counters violent extremism.

The United States must retain a global information capacity as part of the country's international posture. The BBG must meet the challenges posed by state-sponsored media of other countries whose foreign policy aims are often at odds with ours. Chinese and Russian international-facing media organizations, in particular (primarily CCTV and Russia Today), have invested vast sums in expanding influence and reach, especially in Africa, the Arab world, and the Americas, while the Iranian satellite television Press TV aggressively courts audiences in the developing world and the global impact of Qatar's Al Jazeera is well known.

The foremost challenge for the BBG is to deliver programming to audiences via the media and the formats they prefer, despite the instabilities of various broadcast markets. In many cases, the BBG relies on agreements with host country governments to ensure program delivery and access to local radio and TV affiliates. In FY 2014, the BBG established a new FM transmitter in Nouakchott, Mauritania and and launched new programming streams for FMs in Juba, South Sudan and Bangui, Central African Republic. When the political climate or leadership of a country changes, the BBG's ability to continue broadcasting may also change.

To reach audiences, the BBG is constantly working to overcome jamming and censorship. In FY 2014, the BBG launched a joint 24/7 satellite and online stream to China featuring VOA and RFA content in four languages – Mandarin, Cantonese, Tibetan and Uyghur. The BBG has been at the forefront of the battle against satellite jamming, working closely with other concerned parties and through international forums to fight satellite jamming. On behalf of its broadcasters, the BBG's Internet anti-censorship program counteracts activities undertaken by governments such as China and Iran to restrict Internet access, constantly revising and updating its approaches and techniques to thwart Internet censorship.

The BBG must be agile to adjust broadcast media in response to changing media climates.

The BBG responds to crises and political changes worldwide with surges in broadcasting. BBG language services add additional broadcast hours and create rich content to effectively and accurately inform people affected by crises and turmoil with very little lead-time and often with no defined end of surge. As regional and localized crises develop, the BBG must respond quickly and decisively depending on available media resources and the nature of the situation. In FY 2014, as the crisis in the Central African Republic escalated, VOA launched new Sango-language broadcasts. RFE/RL and VOA added new programs in Russian and Ukrainian, in response to events in Ukraine.The geopolitical landscape constantly challenges the BBG to find inventive and dynamic means to achieve its mission. Whether reaching out to populations in crisis, providing a forum for public debate, or engaging the next generation of decision makers, the BBG is continually evaluating its approach and striving to meet the unique challenges that its mission aspires to and that today's global political climate demands.

In June, Radio Sawa launched its Mauritania stream bringing objective and relevant news and information along with a compelling mix of popular Arabic, African and Western music to the people of Mauritania

AUDIENCES

Within this challenging environment, the BBG reaches an unprecedented 215 million people weekly. However, in most countries, audiences skew male and older. Overall, BBG audiences are about 60 percent male, 40 percent female. Many of BBG's target markets have a significant youth bulge. This situation creates an opportunity for BBG networks to expand their audiences and increase their impact by targeting programming and delivery methods to reach key, strategic audiences. Through the Strategy Review process in FY 2014, BBG language services identified key target audiences and associated impact goals.

The Agency's International Audience Research Program assists in this endeavor, both through market research to determine audience interests and assessment of key impact measures. In addition to quantitative surveys, the BBG commissioned 15 qualitative and experimental studies in FY 2014. On the qualitative side, in addition to half a dozen traditional focus group and listener monitoring panel studies, there are half a dozen studies aiming to better understand how audiences use satellite TV, the Internet, social media, and mobile phones. On the experimental studies side, BBG designed three innovative large-scale panel studies with the goal of obtaining insights more frequently and with significantly faster turnaround times than possible with traditional research methods. These include a content panel, and impact panel, and a mobile phone panel.

INFRASTRUCTURE

The BBG requires powerful and reliable broadcast equipment to fulfill its mission. BBG customers – audiences and affiliate stations around the world – often have a number of news choices. To ensure these programs reach target audiences, the BBG must find ways to effectively deliver high quality programs in a format that is preferred by and accessible to the target audience. The BBG must manage a mix of media and technologies from traditional shortwave radio to satellite TV, Internet, and cell phones.

The BBG must carefully manage its transmission infrastructure to maintain a strong presence in critical markets. It is necessary to provide modern and effective transmitting and antenna systems in order to improve signal strength and reliability of broadcasts to vital areas throughout the world. The BBG works to meet this challenge by determining where transmission resources can be best utilized to BBG broadcasts. To make the best use of transmission assets, BBG conducts in-depth analysis to meet the constant challenge of maintaining an effective and cost-effective transmission network.

The rapidly evolving broadcast information technology (IT) market impacts much of the BBG's broadcast and transmission equipment. Different areas of the world depend on different types of broadcast technology, requiring the BBG to maintain a traditional transmission network, while investing in new media technology to support programming efforts such as news delivery via SMS or mobile devices. New infrastructure must be established and maintained along with existing infrastructure, and this maintenance is complicated by the advent of digital technology. While digital technology provides the highest quality production capabilities and increased opportunities for improved efficiencies, digital equipment requires a more stringent replacement and upgrade cycle to meet industry standards. As the pace of obsolescence accelerates with new technologies, vendors discontinue support for older systems and repairs or upgrades become difficult or even impossible. Given these constraints, the BBG strives to judiciously allocate resources to address the most critical infrastructure requirements as well as recurring technical infrastructure requirements and one-time projects.

BBG's Office of Technology, Services, and Innovation has spearheaded a process of migration away from less-effective transmission to platforms that audiences prefer and transfer of transmission from costly facilities to lower-cost options. In FY 2014, the Broadcasting Board of Governors established a Special Committee on the Future of Shortwave Broadcasting to conduct a comprehensive review of the efficacy of shortwave radio as a distribution platform for USIM. The committee found shortwave radio to be essential to listeners in a few target countries, but of marginal impact in most markets. Based on consistent and verifiable data, and audience-based research, it was concluded that shortwave listenership around the world has plummeted, and that shortwave usage does not generally increase during crisis situations. Consequently, BBG has budgeted for the reduction of shortwave transmissions to countries where it is not a viable delivery platform.

BBG's Saipan Transmitting Station

MANAGEMENT

While audience preferences and research dictate the strategies of individual language services across the BBG, the Agency must remain flexible and capable of adapting to changes in regional priorities and broadcast strategies. The BBG must continually assess how best to scale and shape operations, including the right mix of language services, to meet the new challenges while enhancing performance.

Unpredictable global events and changing media consumption habits make it important that the Agency continually improve its ability to respond to events with agility and focus. As audience preferences in target broadcast areas have changed, the BBG has transitioned from radio-only broadcasts to multimedia news and information distribution, including

television, the Internet, text messaging, and mobile applications. Like surge broadcasts, these changes in distribution availability and audience preferences evolve quickly and require that the BBG be innovative to respond effectively and decisively.

Internally, the quality, competence, and morale of the BBG workforce is critical to mission achievement. As such, the Agency has made the development and motivation of its workforce a key component of its Strategic Plan for meeting future challenges. Issues of Federal employee morale and satisfaction, made apparent in the results of federal employee surveys, are being addressed through a comprehensive Workplace Engagement initiative.

The training and development of BBG's dedicated workforce a key component of its Strategic Plan.

Financial Highlights

The BBG financial statements are included in the Financial Section of this report.

The independent accounting firm, Kearney & Company, conducted our FY 2014 financial statement audit and issued an unmodified opinion on our Principal Financial Statements.

Preparing these statements allows the BBG to improve financial management and provide accurate and reliable information to Congress, the President, and the taxpayer. BBG management is responsible for the integrity and objectivity of the financial information presented in the statements.

The financial statements and financial data presented in this report have been prepared from the accounting records of the BBG in conformity with generally accepted accounting principles and incorporate the application of the standards as prescribed by the Federal Accounting Standards Advisory Board.

Financial Highlights *(in thousands)*		2014		2013
At End of the Year:				
Condensed Balance Sheet Data:				
Fund Balance with Treasury	$	191,082	$	161,420
Accounts Receivable		226		112
Advances to Surrogate Broadcasters		55,000		45,576
Property, Plant and Equipment		116,411		118,407
Other		6,324		10,982
Total Assets	$	369,043	$	336,497
Accounts Payable and Other	$	42,038	$	38,815
Retirement and Payroll		40,713		35,665
Total Liabilities	$	82,751	$	74,480
Unexpended Appropriations	$	196,694	$	162,659
Cumulative Results of Operations		89,598		99,358
Total Net Position		286,292		262,017
Total Liabilities and Net Position	$	369,043	$	336,497
For the Year:				
Condensed Statement of Net Cost Data:				
Total Cost	$	728,831	$	743,355
Total Earned Revenue		(3,426)		(3,646)
Total Net Cost of Operations	$	725,405	$	739,709

Management Assurances

FEDERAL MANAGERS' FINANCIAL INTEGRITY ACT (FMFIA)

The Federal Managers' Financial Integrity Act (FMFIA) of 1982 (Public Law 97-255) is designed to provide reasonable assurance that agencies institute management accountability and internal controls that support five objectives:

- **programs achieve their intended results;**

- **resources are effectively used consistent with the Agency's mission;**

- **programs and resources are properly safeguarded against waste, fraud, and mismanagement;**

- **reliable and timely information supports decision making; and**

- **the Agency complies with laws and regulations.**

For compliance with Federal Managers' Financial Integrity Act (FMFIA) of 1982 and Office of Management and Budget (OMB) Circular A-123, Management's Responsibility for Internal Control, revised December 2004; the Agency head of BBG will provide the annual assurance statement on the status of,

- **Internal controls over the effectiveness and efficiency of operations and financial reporting;**

- **Compliance with applicable laws and regulations;**

- **Any reportable conditions or deficiencies that were reported in the financial statements, which are derived from independent audits, Government Accountability Office (GAO), Office of the Inspector General (OIG) reviews, inspections or audits and self-assessments conducted by BBG management;**

FMFIA Section 4 31 U.S.C.3512 (d)(2)(B) (commonly referred to as Section 4 of the Integrity Act) requires that an annual statement on whether an Agency's financial management systems conform with government-wide requirements. If the Agency's systems do not substantially conform to financial system requirements, the statement must list the non-conformances and discuss the Agency's plans for bringing its systems into substantial compliance. Based on this requirement, BBG has to be in compliance with FISMA. It was noted in OIG's FY 2014 FISMA report that BBG had significant deficiency in its enterprise-wide security.

BBG did not evaluate its management controls and financial management systems for FY 2014, in accordance with FMFIA and OMB Circular A-123. As a result of no annual self-assessment, independent audit and OIG acquisition audit, BBG has decided to report no assurance.

FINANCIAL MANAGEMENT SYSTEMS AND REPORTING INTERNAL CONTROL REVIEW

Each year, the Broadcasting Board of Governors receives an independent auditor's report on the internal control and functionality of its financial management systems and platforms. The BBG employs a program to continuously assess, document, and report on internal controls. In addition to safeguarding resources and complying with laws and regulations, the BBG strives to fairly and accurately present financial reports that have a material effect on spending, budgetary, or other financial decisions.

FINANCIAL MANAGEMENT SYSTEMS STRATEGIES

The BBG updated its Momentum financial system interfaces to provide increased functionality and a framework for future enhancements. Performing this update enabled BBG to comply with mandatory Federal Government procurement, accounting, and external reporting changes. These anticipated changes include Treasury's Payment Disbursement Modernization (PAM) and Governmentwide Treasury Account Symbol (GTAS) initiatives, as well as GSA's System for Award Management (SAM) initiative. BBG now has greater processing efficiencies, a solid framework for upcoming requirements, and increased capabilities to remain accurate and accountable.

IMPROPER PAYMENTS PROGRAM

The Broadcasting Board of Governors (BBG) is dedicated to continuing to strengthen its improper payments program to ensure payments are legitimate, processed correctly and efficiently. The Program utilizes an experienced and trained staff, a financial management system that is designed with control functions to mitigate risk, and an internal analysis of processes and transactions.

The BBG conducts the following steps to comply with the Improper Payments Elimination and Recovery Improvement Act of 2012 (IPERIA) and OMB Circular A-123 Appendix C, Part 1:

1. Review all programs and activities and identify those that are susceptible to significant improper payments.

2. Obtain a statistically valid estimate of the annual amount of improper payments for those programs that are identified as susceptible to significant improper payments.

3. Implement a plan to reduce erroneous payments.

4. Report estimates of the annual amount of improper payments in programs and activities and progress in reducing them.

More information on BBG's activities safeguarding against improper payments can be found in Section Four.

FY 2014 Statement of Assurance

INTERNATIONAL BROADCASTING BUREAU

FY 2014 STATEMENT OF ASSURANCE

The Broadcasting Board of Governor's management is responsible for establishing and maintaining effective internal control and financial management systems that meet the objectives of the Federal Managers' Financial Integrity Act (FMFIA). The Broadcasting Board of Governors was unable to conduct its assessment of internal control over programmatic operations in accordance with the Office of Management and Budget (OMB) Circular A-123, *Management's Responsibility for Internal Control* guidelines, due to constraints in resources. Since the assessment of internal controls was not completed, the Broadcasting Board of Governors cannot provide a conclusive assurance of its internal controls over the effectiveness and efficiency of operations and compliance with applicable laws and regulations as of September 30, 2014.

In addition, the Broadcasting Board of Governors was unable to conduct its assessment of the effectiveness of internal control over financial reporting, which includes the safeguarding of assets and compliance with applicable laws and regulations in accordance with the requirements of OMB Circular A-123 due to constraints in resources. Since the assessment of the effectiveness of internal controls was not completed, the Broadcasting Board of Governors cannot provide a conclusive assurance of its internal control over financial reporting as of June 30, 2014, was operating and that no material weaknesses were found in the design or operation of internal control over financial reporting.

BBG has reported three material weakness conditions for FY2013 based on concurrence with the independent audit report. These material weaknesses will not all be fully remediated at the close of FY2014. In addition, the OIG Acquisition audit report dated June 2014 identified significant deficiencies during BBG's Procurement audit. Significant internal control challenges remain at BBG, as we were unable to implement an A-123 internal control assessment program in FY2014. Strong internal controls are critical to BBG's mission, and we plan to have a robust program in place within the FY2015 to FY2016 timeframe. BBG will continue to work collaboratively with OIG on these issues.

Andre Mendes
Director of Global Operations
International Broadcasting Bureau

Suzie Carroll
Director of Global Communications
International Broadcasting Bureau

Robert Bole
Director of Global Strategy
International Broadcasting Bureau

330 Independence Avenue, SW   Washington, DC 20237

Limitations of Financial Statements

The principal financial statements have been prepared to report the financial position and results of operations of the Broadcasting Board of Governors (BBG), pursuant to the requirements of 31 U.S.C. 3515 (b). While the BBG statements have been prepared from its books and records in accordance with Generally Accepted Accounting Principles for Federal entities and the formats prescribed by the Office of Management and Budget, the statements are in addition to the financial reports used to monitor and control budgetary resources, which are prepared from the same books and records.

These statements should be read with the realization that they are for a component of the United States Government, a sovereign entity.

Section 2:
Performance Information

FY 2014 Goals, Objectives, and Results...26

Verification and Validation of Performance Measures..............60

FY 2014 Performance Objectives and Outcomes........................61

Summary of FY 2014 Performance Accomplishments...........64

Use of Performance Data to Promote Improved Outcomes..74

Independent Program Evaluations...76

FY 2014 Goals, Objectives, and Results

SUMMARY OF THE 2014-2018 BBG STRATEGIC PLAN

The BBG's 2014-2018 strategic plan continues an ambitious roadmap to refine and expand the reach and impact of U.S. international media in support of U.S. strategic interests. The plan informs the FY 2016 budget request and continues the integration of performance, budget planning, and management of the BBG.

The mission of the Broadcasting Board of Governors remains to inform, engage, and connect people around the world in support of freedom and democracy.

This mission is achieved through two strategic goals:

- **Expand freedom of information and expression**
- **Communicate America's democratic experience**

Both of these strategic goals serve to further the BBG mission of supporting freedom and democracy. The purpose of communicating America's democratic experience is not merely public diplomacy or "moving the needle"; rather, by presenting a case study in the American experience, we seek to help other countries navigate their own governance challenges.

The BBG's two strategic goals are supported by six strategic objectives and three management objectives, each of which has supporting performance goals. These objectives and goals map out Agency priorities over the next two years.

STRATEGIC AND MANAGEMENT OBJECTIVES

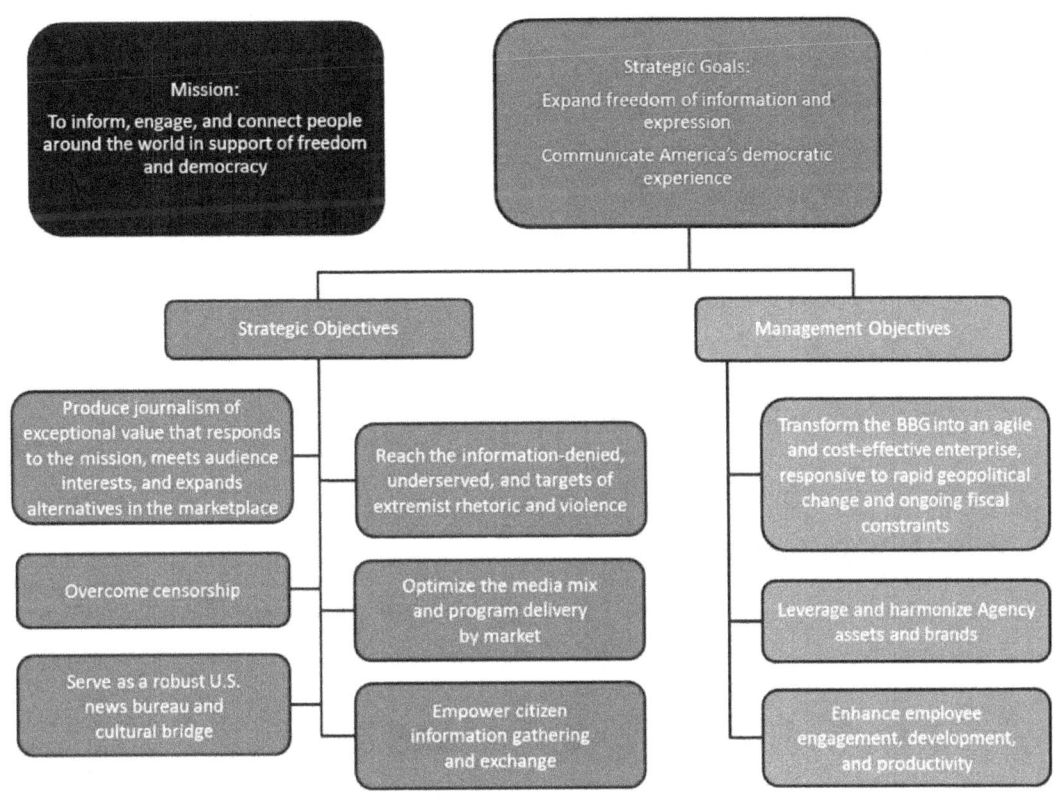

STRATEGIC OBJECTIVE 1:

Produce journalism of exceptional value that responds to the mission, meets audience interests, and expands alternatives in the marketplace

Journalism is the daily work of the BBG broadcasters, and producing fact-based, verifiable news and information must be preeminent in Agency strategy. To have impact, BBG journalism must meet audiences' interests along the breadth of subjects that matter to their lives and, at the same time, must add value in expanding the range of media alternatives. Our aim is not just to follow the 24-hour news cycle but to drive the news agenda through original reporting, in-depth analysis, and a unique cross-cultural perspective that

helps our audiences become sophisticated consumers of news and media.

- As Congressionally mandated, provide news and other programming that is accurate, objective, and comprehensive and in accordance with the highest professional standards of broadcast journalism.

- Produce news and information, consistent with audience preferences and mission requirements, which are not addressed adequately by media in the target area, e.g., human rights and good governance.

- Offer non-news content that research, web analytics, and audience and affiliate feedback show are of vital interest to audiences, such as health, science, and technology.

- Produce enterprise reporting through deep and lasting exploration of critical issues in the countries we target.

- Co-create content with reputable partners, as appropriate and consistent with broadcasting standards and editorial guidelines.

STRATEGIC OBJECTIVE 1: Produce journalism of exceptional value that responds to the mission, meets audience interests, and expands alternatives in the marketplace

Performance Goal 1: Reach significant audiences.

Weekly Listening/Viewing Audiences (in millions)	FY 2010 Actual	FY 2011 Actual	FY 2012 Actual	FY 2013 Actual	FY 2014 Target	FY 2014 Actual
VOA	122.5	141.1	134.2	164.6	167.5	171.6
MBN (Radio Sawa)	17.6	14.9	13.4	11.1	11.5	11.3
MBN (Alhurra)	26.2	26.7	22.9	21.9	23.0	20.9
RFE/RL	18.4	24.3	23.4	17.9	20.2	23.3
RFA	NA	11.9	10.7	10.8	11.0	7.8
OCB	NA	NA	NA	NA	NA	NA

Notes:

- FY 2014 targets are from the FY 2015 Congressional Budget Request.

- MBN figures shown here do not include Afia Darfur, a radio service aimed at the inhabitants of the Darfur region in Sudan. Survey research carried out in Darfur in 2012 indicated that the service had an audience of 1.7 million. If added to the total combined audiences of the other MBN services, Radio Sawa and Alhurra, MBN's total, unduplicated audiences comes to 29.3 million.

- BBG began reporting audience figures for RFA in FY 2011.

INDICATOR:

Regular Listening/ Viewing Audience (Overall Weekly Audiences):

This indicator measures the number of people in target areas listening to or viewing BBG programming or online materials on a weekly basis. The measure is obtained for each language service (except Spanish-to-Cuba, Korean, and Tibetan) and for the countries served by the BBG that were surveyed within the past five years. It is based upon the measurement of the "regular listening audience," a statistical standard long used to report international radio audience reach. Regular listening or viewing audience (radio, TV or Internet) has over the years been consistently defined as all adults listening or viewing at least once a week, as determined by an audience survey that has an adequately designed sample. We do not conduct surveys in every country every year, so reach figures may in some cases reflect weekly reach measures collected from up to five years in the past. This may result in an over or underestimation of actual reach. Additionally, political volatility in certain markets may prevent the measurement of current reach for services broadcasting to these areas.

Analysis of Results:

VOA – Target: 167.5 million   Actual: 171.6 million

With a weekly audience of 171.6 million, VOA exceeded its FY 2014 target of 167.5 million, due to large audience gains in Indonesia. Additional substantial audience gains in Bangladesh, Ukraine, Russia and Cambodia made up for losses in Africa and Burma.

MBN (Radio Sawa) – Target: 11.5 million   Actual: 11.3 million

Radio Sawa's measured audience increased in 2014, and the measured audience of 11.3 million is statistically even with the 11.5 million target.

MBN (Alhurra) – Target: 23.0 million   Actual: 20.9 million

Alhurra's weekly audience declined to 20.9 million in 2014, missing its target of 23.0 million. This drop resulted in part from a decline in reach in Iraq, Alhurra's largest market. Several factors may have contributed to this change. Political conditions have become increasingly volatile in Iraq in the past year and audiences increasingly are turning to partisan news sources rather than relying on media outlets such as Alhurra that present objective news and information.

RFE/RL – Target: 20.2 million   Actual: 23.3 million

After a decline in audience 2013, RFE/RL's weekly audience increased to 23.3 million in 2014, exceeding its target of 20.2 million. The main drivers RFE/RL's recapture of measured global audience were gains in Iran and Ukraine. Audiences in Iran increased nearly 3 million due to the launch of Radio Farda's popular morning program "Breakfast with News" as a television show on VOA's satellite stream, along with higher audiences for radio and Internet products.

RFA – Target: 11.0 million   Actual: 7.8 million

With a weekly audience of 7.8 million, RFA fell short of its target of 11.0 million. The decline was almost entirely due to a drop in audiences in Burma. Previous measurements were done at a time of maximum interest in news in an environment in which very little information was available domestically. With Burma's recent political changes have come a blossoming of local media – more media providers, less overt censorship, more attractive domestic content, and improving infrastructure – combined for many with a less sharp focus on news.

OCB (Radio and TV Martí) – Target: NA   Actual: NA

National estimates of audience reach for OCB in Cuba are not available. Conducting media surveys among probability samples of adults in Cuba has been feasible only via phone, which can reach about 30 percent of adults and remains subject to concerns about underreporting of use of foreign media in a repressive environment. Weekly audiences for Radio and TV Martí measured in such surveys in recent years have consistently been small. In order to gain more detailed and frank information from as many Martí listeners and viewers as possible, BBG commissions surveys and qualitative research among convenience samples of recent Cuban immigrants – whose results cannot be used to estimate audiences in Cuba. The most recent such immigrant study (2012-2013) suggested that, among these respondents, having listened to Radio Martí had been a common experience at some time while they lived in Cuba, while ever having watched TV Martí was relatively rare.

STRATEGIC OBJECTIVE 1: Produce journalism of exceptional value that responds to the mission, meets audience interests, and expands alternatives in the marketplace

Performance Goal 2:

Program Quality – percent of services whose programs are rated "good or better"	FY 2010 Actual	FY 2011 Actual	FY 2012 Actual	FY 2013 Actual	FY 2014 Target	FY 2014 Actual
VOA	100	100	100	100	100	100
MBN (Radio Sawa)	100	NA	NA	NA	100	NA
MBN (Alhurra)	NA	NA	NA	NA	100	NA
RFE/RL	100	96	100	96	100	100
RFA	100	100	100	100	100	100
OCB	100	100	100	100	100	100

Maintain good or excellent program quality ratings for all broadcast services.

INDICATOR:

Program Quality:

This indicator presents the percentage of an entity's language services with programming that is assessed as being of good-or-better quality. Ratings are based upon two broad criteria: (1) *content*, and (2) *presentation*. The *content* criterion includes evaluations of accuracy, reliability, authoritativeness, objectivity, comprehensiveness, and other variables reflecting distinct statutory, policy, and mission mandates for the different stations. The *presentation* criterion involves separate sub-criteria for each production unit unique to its media and the program. Historically, this measure has combined scores of external monitoring panels with the analysis of in-house analysts. With the transition to a new research provider in FY 2012, the BBG is evaluating and restructuring how it conducts external quality analysis. Scores for FY 2012 through 2014 are based exclusively on in-house ratings. Quality scores are summarized on a scale from 1-4, where 1.0-1.3 = poor; 1.4-1.6 = poor to fair; 1.7-2.3 = fair; 2.4-2.6 = fair to good; 2.7-3.3 = good; 3.4-3.6 = good to excellent; 3.7-4.0 = excellent. The percentage of each entity's reviewed language services that fall within the good, good to excellent, or excellent range is then calculated.

Analysis of Results:

VOA – Target: 100   Actual: 100

Program quality ratings continued to be good or excellent for all VOA language services reviewed in FY 2014.

MBN (Radio Sawa) – Target: 100   Actual: NA

A program quality score was not available for Radio Sawa in FY 2014 because quantitative internal reviews were not conducted.

MBN (Alhurra) – Target: 100   Actual: NA

A program quality score was not available for Alhurra in FY 2014 because quantitative internal reviews were not conducted.

RFE/RL – Target: 100   Actual: 100

Program quality ratings continued to be good or excellent for all RFE/RL language services reviewed in FY 2014.

RFA – Target: 100   Actual: 100

Program quality ratings continued to be good or excellent for all RFA language services reviewed in FY 2014.

OCB – Target: 100   Actual: 100

Program quality ratings continued to be good or excellent for all OCB language services reviewed in FY 2014.

Performance Goal 3: Provide programming that audiences find trustworthy.

Program Credibility – percent of weekly audience who consider information to be very or somewhat trustworthy	FY 2010 Actual	FY 2011 Actual	FY 2012 Actual	FY 2013 Actual	FY 2014 Target	FY 2014 Actual
VOA	94	93	92	89	90	89
MBN (Radio Sawa)	90	92	89	85	86	83
MBN (Alhurra)	86	88	84	84	86	84
RFE/RL	92	93	93	92	93	92
RFA	91	92	92	89	91	87
OCB	NA	NA	NA	NA	NA	NA

INDICATOR:

Program Credibility:

This indicator is determined by the survey question about trustworthiness of news and information of those sampled respondents who listened to or viewed each station at least once a week. The answers are registered on a four-point scale – Trust a great deal, Trust it somewhat, Do not trust it very much, Do not trust it at all. The credibility index is the percent of those answering the question in the survey (excluding those who did not respond or did not know) who endorsed trust a great deal or somewhat. Credibility estimates are not included for countries where the number of regular listeners/viewers/online users is so small (n = <50) that the estimate is unreliable.

Analysis of Results:

VOA – Target: 90   Actual: 89

VOA's program credibility score of 89 percent in FY 2014 narrowly missed the target of 90 percent. VOA continues to hold a high level of credibility among its audience with 89 percent of weekly listeners, viewers, and online users rating its programming as very or somewhat trustworthy.

MBN (Radio Sawa) – Target: 86   Actual: 83

MBN Radio Sawa achieved a program credibility score of 83 percent in FY 2014, close to the target of 86 percent. Radio Sawa continues to hold a high level of credibility among listeners with 83 percent of weekly listeners rating its programming as very or somewhat trustworthy.

MBN (Alhurra) – Target: 86   Actual: 84

MBN Alhurra achieved a program credibility score of 84 percent in FY 2014, close to the target of 86 percent. Alhurra continues to hold a high level of credibility among viewers with 84 percent of weekly viewers rating its programming as very or somewhat trustworthy.

RFE/RL – Target: 93   Actual: 92

RFE/RL's program credibility score of 92 percent in FY 2014 barely missed the target of 93 percent. RFE/RL continues to hold a high level of credibility among its audience with 92 percent of weekly listeners, viewers, and online users rating its programming as very or somewhat trustworthy.

RFA – Target: 91   Actual: 87

RFA's program credibility score of 87 percent in FY 2014 did not meet the target of 91 percent. RFA continues to hold a high level of credibility among its audience with 87 percent of weekly listeners, viewers, and online users rating its programming as very or somewhat trustworthy.

OCB – Target: NA   Actual: NA

As previously indicated, the closed nature of Cuban society makes it extraordinarily difficult to conduct surveys or research, and, therefore, program credibility cannot be reliably measured.

STRATEGIC
OBJECTIVE 1:
Produce journalism
of exceptional value
that responds to
the mission, meets
audience interests,
and expands
alternatives in the
marketplace

Performance Goal 4: Provide programming that increases the audiences' understanding of current events.

Understanding – percent of weekly audience who report that the broadcasts have increased their understanding of current events somewhat or a great deal	FY 2010 Actual	FY 2011 Actual	FY 2012 Actual	FY 2013 Actual	FY 2014 Target	FY 2014 Actual
VOA	85	88	88	90	91	90
MBN (Radio Sawa)	70	70	70	80	81	77
MBN (Alhurra)	69	70	72	79	81	77
RFE/RL	85	91	91	90	91	86
RFA	89	83	92	97	91	88
OCB	NA	NA	NA	NA	NA	NA

Note: Because of the limitations of reliable survey data in Cuba, it is not possible to reliably measure understanding for OCB.

INDICATOR:

Understanding of current events:

This indicator is determined by the survey question asking weekly listeners/viewers/online users of [language] whether the broadcasts have "increased their understanding of current events." The answers are registered on a four-point scale – a great deal, somewhat, very little, or not at all. The understanding indicator measures the percent of those answering the question in the survey (excluding those who did not respond or did not know) who chose "a great deal" or "somewhat."

Analysis of Results:

VOA – Target: 91   Actual: 90

VOA's understanding score of 90 percent in FY 2014 fell just shy of the target of 91 percent. VOA continues to increase the understanding of current events among a significant portion of its audience with 90 percent of weekly listeners, viewers, or online users reporting that its programs increased their understanding of current events

MBN (Radio Sawa) – Target: 81   Actual: 77

MBN Radio Sawa's understanding score of 77 percent in FY 2014 was close to the target of 81 percent. Radio Sawa continues to increase the understanding of current events among a significant portion of listeners with 77 percent of weekly listeners reporting that its programs increased their understanding of current events.

MBN (Alhurra) – Target: 81   Actual: 77

MBN Alhurra's understanding score of 77 percent in FY 2014 was close to the target of 81 percent. Alhurra continues to increase the understanding of current events among a significant portion of viewers with 77 percent of weekly viewers reporting that its programs increased their understanding of current events.

RFE/RL – Target: 91   Actual: 86

RFE/RL's understanding score of 86 percent in FY 2014 was close to the target of 91 percent. RFE/RL continues to increase the understanding of current events among a significant portion of its audience with 86 percent of weekly listeners, viewers, or online users reporting that its programs increased their understanding of current events.

RFA – Target: 91   Actual: 88

RFA's understanding score of 88 percent in FY 2014 was close to the target of 91 percent. RFA continues to increase the understanding of current events among a significant portion of its audience with 88 percent of weekly listeners, viewers, or online users reporting that its programs increased their understanding of current events.

OCB – Target: NA   Actual: NA

As previously indicated, the closed nature of Cuban society makes it extraordinarily difficult to conduct surveys or research, and, therefore, understanding cannot be reliably measured.

STRATEGIC
OBJECTIVE 1:
Produce journalism
of exceptional value
that responds to
the mission, meets
audience interests,
and expands
alternatives in the
marketplace

Performance Goal 5: Provide exceptional news and information.

Uniqueness – percent of weekly audience reporting that broadcaster presents information they cannot get from other broadcasters	FY 2014 Target	FY 2014 Actual
VOA		
MBN (Radio Sawa)		
MBN (Alhurra)	Incorporate into core questionnaire	Question has been incorporated into core questionnaire
RFE/RL		
RFA		
OCB		

Note: This is a new measure in FY 2014. Actuals for FY 2010-2013 are not available.

INDICATOR:

Uniqueness:

This indicator is determined by the survey question asking weekly listeners/viewers/online users of any language how much of the information provided by the entity is also available from other sources on the radio, TV, or Internet. The answers are registered on a four-point scale – All of it is available elsewhere, Some of it is available elsewhere, Very little of it is available elsewhere, None of it is available elsewhere. The unique information indicator measures the percent of those answering the question in the survey who chose "very little" or "none."

Analysis of Results:

This question has been incorporated into the core questionnaire. Baselines will be presented for FY 2015 and then targets will be set for subsequent years.

STRATEGIC OBJECTIVE 2:

Reach the information-denied, underserved, and targets of extremist rhetoric and violence

In deciding where to broadcast, BBG considers the local media situation and prioritizes countries that lack a free or developed press. Special consideration is given to populations at risk of violence due to extremist rhetoric. In all target countries, BBG broadcasters seek to grow their audience base and reach those traditionally underserved by our broadcasts. Populations in our target countries are overwhelmingly young – a challenge but also a chance for us to connect with a demographic that in the main has never even heard of us. Our current audiences are approximately 60 percent male and 40 percent female – an imbalance ripe for correcting. We understand that to reach and be relevant with these audiences we need to provide them with content that not only informs them of international and local news, but assists them in building and participating in a civil society. BBG pays special attention to audiences in areas plagued by extremism, as extremist forces espouse a violent ideology and execute campaigns of terror that threaten U.S. and regional security and stymie free, open, democratic societies. Support for programming to these audiences is in the interests of U.S. national security.

- Prioritize countries lacking freedom and democracy or faced with extremism where accurate, credible news and information are lacking; boost service to these areas, where feasible.

- Introduce service in selected new languages to reach sizeable new audiences in important countries where our products are urgently needed.

- Reach out to women and youth with the kinds of content and conversation they wish to have beyond traditional news and information paradigms.

- Sharpen audience segmentation and targeting to drive content strategies and better address gender and age demographics, as well as psychographic segments.

- Create country-specific content streams in existing languages to augment news and information for priority countries, e.g., Egypt, Mali.

- Serve as a conduit for the transmission of reporting from inside closed societies to outside audiences.

- Ensure strong local news coverage, as warranted by events, to meet urgent audience needs in areas of crisis.

- Draw on the experiences of the world's many models of free societies, in particular the U.S., to present a broad array of political views and debates.

STRATEGIC
OBJECTIVE 2:
Reach the
information-denied,
underserved, and
targets of extremist
rhetoric and
violence

Performance Goal 1:
Increase audience reach in environments subject to extremist violence.

	FY 2014 Baseline
Increase weekly audience in Francophone Africa[1]	8.9 million
Increase weekly audience in Anglophone Africa[2]	33.0 million
Increase weekly reach in Kenya	6.0% (Oct 2013)
Increase weekly reach in Tanzania	20.3% (Sep 2012)
Increase weekly reach in Nigeria	16.9% (Mar 2014)
Increase weekly reach in Niger	16.0% (Dec 2013)
Increase weekly radio audience in capital cities where BBG operates an FM transmitter[3]	Accra, Ghana: 4.8% Abidjan, Cote d'Ivoire: 14.5% Bamako, Mali: 7.6% Bangui, Central African Republic: 15.3% Freetown, Sierra Leone: 6.2% Hargeisa, Somalia: 41.3% Juba, South Sudan: 27.7% Kigali, Rwanda: 46.5% Nairobi, Kenya: 5.2% N'Djamena, Chad: 44.1% Nouakchott, Mauritania: no data Ougadougou, Burkina Faso: 9.9%[4] Sao Tome, Sao Tome and Principe: no data
Increase weekly audience reach in DRC (beyond reach of VOA French and Swahili)	7.0% (Nov 2012)

[1]Survey dates: Benin (Jun 2013); Burkina Faso (May 2013); Burundi (Mar 2010); Cameroon (Apr 2013); Central African Republic (Nov 2012); Chad (Oct 2012); Congo, Brazzaville (Jun 2013); Congo, Kinshasa (Nov 2012); Cote d'Ivoire (Jan 2014); Guinea (Dec 2009); Mali (Dec 2013); Rwanda (May 2012); Senegal (May 2013).

[2]Survey dates: Ghana (Nov 2013); Kenya (Oct 2013); Liberia (Sep 2012); Nigeria (Mar 2014); Sierra Leone (Mar 2010); Somalia (Feb 2013); South Africa (Dec 2012); South Sudan (Apr 2012); Tanzania (Sep 2012); Uganda (Jul2012); Zambia (Jun 2013).

[3]Survey dates are the same as above.

[4]Reach in Ougadougou, Burkina Faso reflects radio and television audiences; it cannot be disaggregated.

INDICATOR:

Weekly audience is defined under Strategic Objective 1, Performance Goal 1.

Analysis of Results:

Baselines for FY 2014 are presented here. Targets are set for FY 2015 and 2016.

	FY 2014 Baseline
Expand weekly audience reach in Burma	11.2% (Mar 2014)
Expand weekly audience reach in Cambodia	30.8% (Jun 2014)
Expand weekly audience reach in Vietnam	1.9% (Mar 2013)
Expand digital audience reach in China	0.03% (Nov 2009)

STRATEGIC OBJECTIVE 2: Reach the information-denied, underserved, and targets of extremist rhetoric and violence

Performance Goal 2:

Increase audience reach in environments lacking information.

INDICATOR:

Weekly audience is defined under Strategic Objective 1, Performance Goal 1.

Analysis of Results:

Baselines for FY 2014 are presented here. Targets are set for FY 2015 and 2016.

Contextual Indicators:

	# of BBG target countries ranked		
2014 Freedom House Rankings	**Not Free**	**Partly Free**	**Free**
Freedom of the Press	62	51	7
Freedom in the World (political)	48	49	23

STRATEGIC OBJECTIVE 3: **Overcome Censorship**

For almost 70 years U.S. international broadcasting has fought censorship in all its forms. Today, as the global media environment undergoes a dynamic revolution, access to a truly free press is actually in decline. Jamming of radio and TV broadcasts, including our own, continues in a number of countries. Journalists suffer harassment and violence daily. Media laws often restrict free flows of information, limiting the ability of international news organizations to distribute their content. The Internet in particular is under assault. The Agency upholds the universal right of citizens everywhere to receive and impart information without restriction. We work on many fronts to make news and information accessible to our global audiences with the aim of enabling not only unfettered access to our own products but also the full spectrum of independent news sources on the Internet.

- Lead in assisting the world's citizens to gain access to information on all platforms, advocating on the international stage and coordinating within the U.S. government and with international broadcasters and other allies.

- Help audiences understand through journalistic reports the practices and policies of Internet censorship and circumvention.

- Fund technologies that counter Internet censorship and Internet blocking.

- Increase effective use of social media and digital platforms to combat censorship.

- Provide in-house digital expertise to address real-time censorship and jamming issues in targeted regions.

Performance Goal 1:
Increase traffic through Internet Anti-Censorship products

	FY 2010 Actuals	FY 2011 Actuals	FY 2012 Actual	FY 2013 Actual	FY 2014 Target	FY 2014 Actual
Increase proxy traffic through Ultrasurf	NA	NA	19,210 TB	20,000 TB	21,000 TB	21,900 TB
Increase proxy traffic through Psiphon	NA	NA	420 TB	1,961 TB	3,000 TB	4,125 TB
Increase Satellite Internet traffic to Cuba	NA	NA	24 GB	138 GB	180 GB	17 GB

STRATEGIC OBJECTIVE 3: Overcome censorship

Note: Internet anti-censorship products supported by RFA's Open Technology Fund are not represented here. Performance goals for these products have not yet been established.

INDICATORS:
Proxy Traffic through Ultrasurf:

This indicator measures the volume of Internet traffic through the Ultrasurf, a BBG-supported proxy tool for circumventing Internet censorship.

Proxy Traffic through Psiphon:

This indicator measures the volume of Internet traffic through the Psiphon, a BBG-supported proxy tool for circumventing Internet censorship.

Satellite Internet Traffic to Cuba:

This indicator measures the volume of Internet traffic through BBG's satellite Internet link to Cuba.

Analysis of Results:

Proxy Traffic through Ultrasurf – Target: 21,000 TB   Actual: 21,900 TB

With 21,900 TB of traffic in FY 2014, proxy traffic through Ultrasurf exceeded its target of 21,000 TB.

Proxy Traffic through Psiphon – Target: 3,000 TB   Actual: 4,125 TB

With 4,125 TB of traffic in FY 2014, proxy traffic through Psiphon exceeded its target of 3,000 TB even with an aggressive censorship initiative by the Iranian government to specifically block Psiphon traffic in June.

Satellite Internet Traffic to Cuba – Target: 180 GB   Actual: 17 GB

In FY 2014, satellite Internet traffic to Cuba decreased markedly due to contractual limitations on bandwidth. Bandwidth ran out in 2013 and people stopped using the system. Since acquiring new bandwidth, users have been slow to return. It is hoped that given time and increased funding, numbers can return to the initial growth rate.

Contextual Indicator:

2013 Freedom House Rankings	# of BBG target countries ranked	
	Not Free	Partly Free
Freedom on the Net	8	3

STRATEGIC OBJECTIVE 4:

Optimize the media mix and program delivery by market

It is essential that we reach audiences on their preferred media platforms. Yet the Agency's distribution methods and means have lagged shifts in media use. We must therefore align how we deliver our content with how consumers now access it. For traditional media, we must migrate to the most effective broadcast channels, including satellite TV and FM radio. We must accelerate our investment into growing and enhancing new distribution methods, with specific attention to social and mobile platforms. And considering we have one of the world's largest affiliate networks, we must aggressively expand and improve our affiliations and syndication of content in effective formats. Ultimately, the Agency is platform-agnostic. We seek to do what works best for the market at hand to get our content to as many users as possible.

- Increase distribution on platforms that we know audiences are using – FM, satellite TV, and mobile devices – migrating away from legacy platforms where they do not reach audiences.

- Find creative ways to penetrate closed societies, through flash drives, DVDs, and other alternative delivery means.

- Expand local distribution through affiliation with strong local television and FM radio stations and, where possible, installation of FM transmitters.

- Exploit the falling cost of video production by updating our broadcasting facilities to support growing audience appetite for TV and video. Support audience's growing appetite for social media, TV, and video by purchasing equipment and rebuilding aging infrastructure and broadcasting facilities.

- Draw on research and other inputs to tailor formal and presentation styles to audience needs and media usage habits, creating content that can break through ever increasing clutter.

- Integrate and digitize all content – e.g. text, audio, photos, graphics, and video – on a common content management system to facilitate use across platforms, support on-demand needs of the audience, and increase use via syndication.

Performance Goal 1: Increase web and mobile traffic.

Total weekly visitors to web and mobile sites	FY 2014 Target	FY 2014 Actual
VOA	Roll out new analytics tool and establish baselines	2,700,900
MBN (Alhurra)		135,978
MBN (Sawa)		145,873
RFE/RL		2,628,500
RFA		435,100
OCB		50,400

STRATEGIC OBJECTIVE 4: Optimize the media mix and program delivery by market

Note: In FY 2014, the BBG made an investment in enterprise-quality digital analytical systems to provide a digital measurement and insights across all of its websites and mobile applications. This switch resulted in data discontinuity that required rebaselining in FY 2014. VOA, RFE/RL, RFA, and OCB numbers are provisional based on the initial configuration of the new analytics tool. This configuration was audited, and determined to have some technical flaws in setup which may have affected the numbers collected. These flaws have been addressed, but the outcome of the changes is unknown. If this or subsequent corrections to the configuration change the numbers significantly, IBB will rebaseline all the entities in FY 15. MBN numbers are from the legacy analytics tool.

INDICATOR:

Average weekly visitors:

This indicator measures the number of unique web browsers or computers that load BBG websites and mobile websites.

This is calculated weekly, and averaged over the fiscal year.

Analysis of Results:

A new analytics tool has been rolled out and baselines for FY 2014 are shown above. Targets are set for FY 2015 and 2016.

STRATEGIC OBJECTIVE 4: Optimize the media mix and program delivery by market

Performance Goal 2: Build strong affiliate relationships.

Number of affiliations (broadcast, online, and mobile)	FY 2010 Actual	FY 2011 Actual	FY 2012 Actual	FY 2013 Actual	FY 2014 Target	FY 2014 Actual
VOA	360	371	383	2,252	2,400	1,838
RFE/RL	62	65	81	759	287	528
RFA	7	7	14	29	30	23

Note: In FY 2013, the BBG changed its methodology for counting affiliates. This stemmed, in part, from an upgrade to its affiliate database to promote better communication with affiliates, as well as the growing importance of digital outlets. Where previously only high impact, high quality radio and TV affiliates with signed contracts were tallied, the affiliation indicator now counts all stations or outlets that regularly retransmit content from BBG networks. The methodology for counting affiliates was further refined in FY 2014. 1,838 affiliates for VOA includes 1,411 Affiliates, 33 Stations owned by BBG transmitting programming from VOA, and 394 Affiliates to the "Direct" newsfeed service. Previous estimates for RFE were undercounted.

INDICATOR:

Affiliations:

Affiliates are a primary gatekeeper between the BBG networks and their end users – the audiences that listen, watch, and read their content online, on mobile and by broadcast outlets. Counting the number of affiliates, then, offers a measure of the appeal of the programming to these vital gatekeepers and distributors of the BBG networks' content. As shortwave usage wanes in parts of the world, the importance of affiliations with local medium wave and

FM radio and television stations grows. With the growth of digital and mobile technology, there are new forms of affiliations, including online and mobile. In FY 2013, the BBG changed its methodology for counting affiliates. This stemmed, in part, from an upgrade to its affiliate database to promote better communication with affiliates, as well as the growing importance of digital outlets. Where previously only high impact, high quality radio and TV affiliates with signed contracts were tallied, the affiliation indicator now counts all stations or outlets that regularly retransmit content from BBG networks.

Analysis of Results:

VOA Affiliates – Target: 2,400   Actual: 1,838

Due to the methodology change for counting affiliates described above, VOA's affiliates in FY 2014 cannot meaningfully be compared to the target previously established. Targets for FY 2015 and beyond will be established on this new baseline.

RFE/RL Affiliates – Target: 287   Actual: 528

Due to the methodology change for counting affiliates described above, RFE/RL's affiliates in FY 2014 cannot meaningfully be compared to the target previously established. Targets for FY 2015 and beyond will be established on this new baseline.

RFA Affiliates – Target: 30   Actual: 23

Due to the methodology change for counting affiliates described above, RFA's affiliates in FY 2014 cannot meaningfully be compared to the target previously established. Targets for FY 2015 and beyond will be established on this new baseline.

STRATEGIC OBJECTIVE 5:

Serve as a robust U.S. news bureau and cultural bridge

Representing American society and presenting and discussing U.S. policy are legislated mandates for the Agency and thus constitute mission imperatives. BBG coverage of the U.S. is comprehensive across all elements of society but aims overall to convey the practice of democracy in all of its complexity. It is not about persuading audiences to like us; it is about helping them see how we manage the challenges of our democratic society – from economic growth to fiscal crises to race relations to educating our youth to addressing environmental change. These topic areas find ready comparisons in our target countries and resonate with our audiences in practical, meaningful ways. Carrying them out requires sensitivity and creativity. Currents of anti-Americanism still run strong in some parts of the world, necessitating deft outreach on our part that stresses dialogue not monologue. The way people interact with media today, with emphasis on interaction, further affirms this approach. At the same time, America's still dominant role on the global stage makes our country a focal point of international attention, and our national language is the one that tens of millions of people around the world seek to learn. VOA, in particular, is uniquely mandated and positioned to leverage these advantages to connect with diverse international audiences, serving as a U.S. news bureau for our affiliate partners and providing English-learning programming.

- Serve as a U.S. bureau for media outlets across the world that wish to engage with us for news, analysis, and perspectives from the United States – on the model that has

succeeded in Armenia, Bolivia, Turkey, et al.

- Emphasize English learning as a vehicle for positive audience engagement and interaction as well as information on American society and culture.

- Meet the global interest in American politics with in-depth coverage and analysis of national elections and coverage of other political events to impart the news and to elucidate the democratic process, with stories localized to make them interesting to specific target regions.

- Satisfy the world's growing appetite for learning English through TV and radio programs, online instruction, printed instructional materials, and innovative short-form videos posted on the Web.

STRATEGIC OBJECTIVE 5: Serve as a robust U.S. news bureau and cultural bridge

Performance Goal 1: Provide programming that increases audiences' understanding of the United States.

Understanding of American society – percent of weekly audience who report that the broadcasts have increased their understanding of U.S. society somewhat or a great deal	FY 2014 Target	FY 2014 Actual
VOA	Establish baselines	66
MBN (Radio Sawa)		48
MBN (Alhurra)		47

Note: This is a new measure in FY 2014. Actuals from FY 2010-2013 are not available. Baselines for this measure are based on a very small sample of countries—mainly those surveyed in 2013/2014.

Understanding of U.S. foreign policy – percent of weekly audience who report that the broadcasts have increased their understanding of U.S. foreign policy somewhat or a great deal	FY 2014 Target	FY 2014 Actual
VOA		64
MBN (Radio Sawa)	Establish baselines	41
MBN (Alhurra)		46

Note: This is a new measure in FY 2014. Actuals from FY 2010-2013 are not available. Baselines for this measure are based on a very small sample of countries—mainly those surveyed in 2013/2014.

INDICATORS:

Understanding of American Society:

This indicator is determined by the survey question asking weekly listeners/viewers/online users of a BBG entity's broadcasts in a particular language whether the broadcasts have "increased their understanding of American society." The answers are registered on a four-point scale – a great deal, somewhat, very little, or not at all. The understanding indicator measures the percent of those answering the question in the survey (excluding those who did not respond or did not know) who chose "a great deal" or "somewhat."

Understanding of U.S. Foreign Policy:

This indicator is determined by the survey question asking weekly listeners/viewers/online users of a BBG entity's broadcasts in a particular language whether the broadcasts have "increased their understanding of U.S. foreign policy." The answers are registered on a four-point scale – a great deal, somewhat, very little, or not at all. The understanding indicator measures the percent of those answering the question in the survey (excluding those who did not respond or did not know) who chose "a great deal" or "somewhat."

Analysis of Results:

Baselines for FY 2014 are presented here. Targets are set for FY 2015 and 2016.

STRATEGIC OBJECTIVE 6:

Empower citizen information gathering and exchange

New and powerful web, mobile, and social media tools are enabling increasingly diverse voices to be heard around the world. These tools have made media personal, moving the power from centralized broadcasters to a new class of bloggers, activists, videographers, and a content-generating public. They are using media not only to tell their stories on a digital world stage but also to connect with one another to chart the future of their communities and build new forms of civil society. Social media are also changing the way news is gathered and distributed, requiring news organizations to adopt new work flows that allow them to use multiple platforms to deliver content to a global audience. Our Agency must aggressively pursue an innovation agenda that develops the next generation of content, tools, and distribution platforms.

- Nurture citizen journalism and channel user-generated content from inside repressive states.

- Link citizens within repressive societies and to external audiences through social media networks.

- Facilitate dialogue across religious, national and ethnic groups.

- Enter into a "global conversation" with our audiences by using social media tools to identify, source, and distribute news content into the channels where people are having conversations about their community and the world.

- Build new partnerships to create tools that help us more efficiently and effectively translate content for a global audience around high-quality news and information.

- Pursue partnerships with technologists around the globe who are building the next generation of digital media technology through mobile and social media.

- Develop a suite of new media products that can be easily deployed by language services based on market consumption data, with an eye toward maximizing opportunities for user generated content, peer-to-peer sharing, and audience interactivity.

Performance Goal 1: Increase audience interaction via social media.

Digital Engagement Impact Index	FY 2014 Target	FY 2014 Actual
VOA		
MBN	Systematic, automated collection of social media data to establish baselines.	System for automated collection of social media data rolled out in Q4 FY 2014.
RFE/RL		
RFA		
OCB		

STRATEGIC OBJECTIVE 6: Empower citizen information gathering and exchange

Note: This is a new measure in FY 2014. Actuals from FY 2010-2013 are not available.

INDICATOR:

Digital Engagement Impact Index:

This indicator measures the total number of engagement actions on currently measurable platforms, currently Facebook and Twitter. Engagement actions include measurable actions that demonstrate an activity beyond just consuming content: liking or favoriting a BBG post, commenting on a BBG post, sharing a BBG post, @mentioning a BBG account (Twitter only), liking or following a BBG account or profile.

Analysis of Results:

With the rollout of the new automated system for collecting social media data in FY 2014, the BBG met this goal and will begin baselining the digital engagement impact index in FY 2015.

STRATEGIC
OBJECTIVE 6:
Empower citizen
information
gathering and
exchange

Performance Goal 2: Increase sharing of BBG programming.

Percent of weekly audience who shared something heard/read/seen on broadcaster weekly	FY 2014 Target	FY 2014 Actual
VOA		54
MBN (Radio Sawa)		NA
MBN (Alhurra)	Establish baselines	NA
RFE/RL		48
RFA		55
OCB		NA

Note: This is a new measure in FY 2014. Actuals from FY 2010-2013 are not available. Baselines for this measure are based on a very small sample of countries—mainly those surveyed in 2013/2014.

INDICATOR:

Sharing of programming:

This indicator is determined by the survey question asking weekly listeners/viewers/online users in any language how often they share news that they have heard, seen, or read from a BBG entity with friends or relatives, or with their social network. The answers are registered on a five-point range – Daily or most days per week, At least once a week, At least once a month, Less than once a month, Never. The sharing indicator measures the percent of those answering the question in the survey who chose "Daily or most days per week" or "At least once a week."

Analysis of Results:

Baselines for FY 2014 are presented here. Targets are set for FY 2015 and 2016.

MANAGEMENT OBJECTIVE 1:

Transform the BBG into an agile and cost-effective enterprise, responsive to rapid geopolitical change and ongoing fiscal constraints

By virtual of historical circumstance, today's BBG is a complex amalgam of diverse media outlets and respective support organizations, operating under different legal and administrative frameworks. The result is an organization lacking the agility essential to operate in a rapidly evolving global media environment and the standardization that enables rational resource allocations. Going forward, the Agency must undergo rapid and fundamental transformation in order to appropriately fulfill its charter amidst growing geo-political instability and substantial budgetary challenges.

- Restructure Agency management by appointing an Agency-wide CEO to manage the Agency's day-to-day operations, with a part-time board of directors focused on strategy, budget, and public outreach.

- Enhance the Agency's technological platforms and workflows enabling it to continually adapt to global standards in content acquisition, manipulation, distribution, and audience consumption behaviors.

- Transform workplace and increase collaboration by leveraging open space concepts.

- Make innovation a core value of how we work and interface with audiences and other stakeholders.

- Automate and streamline business processes and work flows.

Performance Goal 1: Restructure Agency management

	FY 2014 Target	FY 2014 Actual
Pursue CEO appointment	Engage CEO search firm	CEO selected

INDICATOR:
CEO appointment:

This goal presented milestones along the way to a CEO appointment.

Analysis of Results:

CEO appointment – Target – search firm engaged; Actual – CEO selected

The BBG exceeded this target, meeting FY 2014 and 2015 goals, with the selection of a CEO in FY 2014. The Agency is currently in the process of bringing him on board.

MANAGEMENT
OBJECTIVE 1:
Transform the BBG
into an agile and
cost-effective
enterprise,
responsive to rapid
geopolitical change
and ongoing fiscal
constraints

Performance Goal 2: Enhance the Agency's technological posture

	FY 2014 Target	FY 2014 Actual
Execute seamless transition to Internet and fiber optic content distribution to stations and uplinks	All owned satellite uplinks fed via global MPLS network.	MPLS infrastructure put in place to facilitate satellite optimization. MPLS has replaced leased fiber optic cables. 80% of owned uplink facilities have MPLS connectivity.

Note: This is a new measure in FY 2014. Actuals from FY 2010-2013 are not available.

INDICATOR:

Satellite uplinks fed by MPLS:

This indicator measures the percentage of satellite uplinks in the global BBG network that are fed by MPLS (Multiprotocol Label Switching).

Analysis of Results:

Satellite uplinks fed by MPLS – Target: 100%   Actual 80%

Although the BBG made great progress against this goal, it achieved 80% of satellite uplinks fed by MPLS, falling short of the target of 100%. Connectivity to the Kuwait Transmitting Station has been challenging due to high costs and limited availability. The BBG is currently looking at both fiber and microwave connectivity from downtown Kuwait City to station.

MANAGEMENT
OBJECTIVE 1:
Transform the BBG
into an agile and
cost-effective
enterprise,
responsive to rapid
geopolitical change
and ongoing fiscal
constraints

Performance Goal 3: Transform workplace and increase collaboration

	FY 2014 Target	FY 2014 Actual
Leverage open space concepts	15% of total footprint	41% of total footprint

Note: This is a new measure in FY 2014. Actuals from FY 2010-2013 are not available.

INDICATOR:

Open space:

This indicator measures the percentage of the total footprint of BBG headquarters that is configured as open space.

Analysis of Results:

Open space – Target: 15%   Actual 41%

With 41% of the headquarters configured as open space in FY 2014, BBG exceeded the target of 15%. Future gains will be constrained by the fact that 33% of the total footprint is technical space not suitable for open space concepts, e.g., conference rooms, data rooms, and broadcasting studios.

Performance Goal 4: Make innovation a core value

	FY 2014 Target	FY 2014 Actual
Ensure managers undertake innovative projects (measured by prototype or proof of concept projects for improving internal management, communication, or media strategy)	15% of supervisory positions undertake and report on new innovative activities	NA

MANAGEMENT OBJECTIVE 1: Transform the BBG into an agile and cost-effective enterprise, responsive to rapid geopolitical change and ongoing fiscal constraints

INDICATOR:
Innovation:

This indicator measures the percentage of supervisory positions that undertake and report on new innovative activities.

Analysis of Results:

This goal was determined to be unmeasurable and has been rescinded.

The BBG remains committed innovation in management, communications, and media strategy and will work on developing more measurable goals around innovation in the future.

MANAGEMENT
OBJECTIVE 1:
Transform the BBG
into an agile and
cost-effective
enterprise,
responsive to rapid
geopolitical change
and ongoing fiscal
constraints

Performance Goal 5: Automate and streamline key business processes

	FY 2014 Target	FY 2014 Actual
Complete business process reengineering and automation of business and media workflows	Automate Time and Attendance system; Complete analysis of Financial, HR and Payroll systems integration	Automated Time and Attendance system has been delayed due to unavailability of funds; Analysis of Financial, HR and Payroll systems substantially underway and on track for completion in Q1 FY 2015

Note: This is a new measure in FY 2014. Actuals from FY 2010-2013 are not available.

INDICATOR:

Business process reengineering and automation:

This goal presents milestones related to reengineering and automating key business processes.

Analysis of Results:

Time and attendance system automation

This milestone was not accomplished in FY 2014, due to lack of available funds. It has been moved to FY 2015.

Analysis of Financial, HR, and Payrolls systems integration

This milestone was substantially underway in FY 2014 and is on track for completion in the first quarter of FY 2015.

MANAGEMENT OBJECTIVE 2:

Leverage and harmonize Agency assets and brands

The BBG is one of the world's largest news-gathering and reporting enterprises with more than 80 language services, 50 overseas news bureaus, 4,000 employees, and 1,500 stringer reporters. Each of the Agency's five broadcasters generates original reporting every day from and around the world's hotspots – the Sahel and Central Africa, Afghanistan-Pakistan border region, Burma, China, Egypt, Iran, North Korea, Russia, Syria, Yemen, et al – primarily in vernacular languages for target audiences in these areas. Too little of this rich content is translated and shared across the BBG to augment international news coverage for other BBG vernacular services or made available to other global audiences in English. BBG will remedy this by facilitating coordination between broadcast entities and reinforcing their unique and respective mission-driven legislated roles in areas served by multiple broadcasters.

- Ensure coordinated and complementary mission-driven operations and content served by two BBG media entities.

- Build the internal content-sharing network, aligning internal editorial support and coordination, as needed.

- Channel original reporting from the language services to the central

newsrooms and across the BBG to get maximum mileage out of the content we currently produce.

- Harmonize news gathering, including stringer and correspondent networks, across the BBG to ensure required editorial coordination and avoid redundancy.

- Use our coordinated news gathering and reporting structures as assets to provide affiliates with greater value, through interactive segments and other special offerings.

- Research and develop translation capacities, partnering, as appropriate, with outside organizations to access expertise and resources, as needed.

Performance Goal 1:
Develop coordinated strategies, operational plans, and budgets for BBG language services in countries/regions served by more than one network

	FY 2014 Target	FY 2014 Actual
Establish shared strategies, operational plans, and budgets; enter evidence into SMART (Strategic Management and Audience Research Tool)	Eurasian markets served by VOA and RFE/RL	Shared strategies and plans for Iran, Ukraine, Caucasus, and Balkans

MANAGEMENT OBJECTIVE 2: Leverage and harmonize agency assets and brands

Note: This is a new measure in FY 2014. Actuals from FY 2010-2013 are not available.

INDICATOR:
Harmonization:

This goal marks progress in coordinating strategies, operational plans, and budgets across BBG entities that serve the same countries or regions.

Analysis of Results:

Harmonization – Target: Eurasian markets
Actual: Iran, Ukraine, Caucasus, and Balkans

In FY 2014, BBG initiated an intensive effort to harmonize operations in several key markets. Significant progress has been made in broadcasts to Iran, Ukraine, the Caucasus and the Balkans, meeting this performance goal.

MANAGEMENT OBJECTIVE 2: Leverage and harmonize agency assets and brands

Performance Goal 2:
Increase the quantity of original reporting shared across language services

	FY 2014 Target	FY 2014 Actual
Share content across language services	Establish baseline for shared content on common systems (Pangea, Direct, Dalet, and News Share)	Various systems in place for sharing among language services and entities (e.g., News Share, VOA Insights, RFE/RL Editorial Agenda). Tracking systems and baselining moved to FY 15 target.

Note: This is a new measure in FY 2014. Actuals from FY 2010-2013 are not available.

INDICATOR:
Content shared across language services:

This indicator measures the quantity of BBG content that is shared across language services, both within and across entities.

Analysis of Results:

The BBG has put in place various systems and communication tools for sharing content across language services, including NewsShare, VOA Insights, and RFE/RL's Editorial Agenda. While there is anecdotal evidence that these systems have increased coordination and sharing of content, there are currently no tracking mechanisms to measure this systematically.

MANAGEMENT OBJECTIVE 3:

Enhance employee engagement, development, and productivity

Our diverse, multi-cultural, and multi-talented workforce offers a rich range of experience and expertise to carry out the Agency's mission. Key to success in a rapidly changing, highly competitive global media environment is flexibility to develop innovative products for our target countries consistent with emerging priorities, programming formats, and advances in technology. Enhanced skill sets are required to program for and transmit via multiple media platforms – radio, TV, Internet, mobile, and though social media. Our employees are most effective when they are well motivated, trained, and led. Continued efforts to equip and energize the entire BBG workforce are critical as we confront mounting competitive pressures worldwide.

- Promote human capital planning and management as a top priority for senior executives, managers, and supervisors throughout the agency.

- Consistently communicate organizational goals, objectives, priorities, and performance expectations in a timely manner to staff at all levels in the agency.

- Ensure a safe and secure work environment for all employees.

- Implement manager training curriculum focusing on performance management, human capital planning and processes, communication, and financial and administrative management.

- Improve the consistency and credibility of agency performance management processes.

- Develop cross-training and internal development standards and procedures, as applicable.

- Foster employee participation in agency health and wellness programs.

Performance Goal 1: Improve performance culture of agency.

Results-oriented performance culture index (from Federal Employee Viewpoint Survey)	FY 2010 Actual	FY 2011 Actual	FY 2012 Actual	FY 2013 Actual	FY 2014 Target	FY 2014 Actual
BBG	NA	NA	46	46	46	44
Government-wide (for comparison)	NA	NA	52	51		51

MANAGEMENT OBJECTIVE 3: Enhance employee engagement, development and productivity

INDICATOR:

Results-oriented Performance Culture Index:

This indicator is an index derived from the Federal Employee Viewpoint Survey and combines questions dealing with recognition, supervision, safety, work connection, and performance.

Analysis of Results:

Results-oriented Performance Culture Index – Target: 46   Actual: 44

The BBG did not meet the target for results-oriented performance culture index in FY 2014, achieving only 44 versus the target of 46.

MANAGEMENT OBJECTIVE 3: Enhance employee engagement, development and productivity

Performance Goal 2: Improve employee training and development.

Percentage of employees who believe that the workforce has the job-relevant knowledge and skills necessary to accomplish organizational goals (from Federal Employee Viewpoint Survey)	FY 2010 Actual	FY 2011 Actual	FY 2012 Actual	FY 2013 Actual	FY 2014 Target	FY 2014 Actual
BBG	56	59	53	55	55	53
Government-wide (for comparison)	NA	NA	72	70		69

INDICATOR:

Workforce Knowledge and Skills:

This indicator is taken from the Federal Employee Viewpoint Survey and measures the percentage of employees with positive responses to the statement that the workforce has the job-relevant knowledge and skills necessary to accomplish organizational goals.

Analysis of Results:

Workforce Knowledge and Skills – Target: 55   Actual: 53

The BBG did not meet the target for knowledge and skills in FY 2014, achieving only 53 percent versus the target of 55 percent.

Performance Goal 3: Increase participation in Health and Wellness Program.

Percentage of employees participating in Health and Wellness program (from Federal Employee Viewpoint Survey)	FY 2010 Actual	FY 2011 Actual	FY 2012 Actual	FY 2013 Actual	FY 2014 Target	FY 2014 Actual
BBG	NA	10	11	26	30	25

MANAGEMENT OBJECTIVE 3: Enhance employee engagement, development and productivity

INDICATOR:

Health and Wellness Participation:

This indicator is taken from the Federal Employee Viewpoint Survey and measures the percentage of employees who participate in the Agency's Health and Wellness program.

Analysis of Results:

Health and Wellness Participation – Target: 30   Actual: 25

The BBG did not meet the target for knowledge and skills in FY 2014, achieving only 53 percent versus the target of 55 percent.

Verification and Validation of Performance Measures

The performance indicators are a best effort to measure each broadcast entity's performance level. To achieve maximum objectivity, measurements are performed independently of the elements being evaluated whenever possible. The VOA, OCB, RFE/RL, RFA, and MBN audience research for the fiscal years reported was carried out by outside research providers under contract to the BBG, currently Gallup. Network-wide performance values are computed by the IBB Office of Research and verified by each network's research director.

The standards of the Conference of International Broadcasting Audience Researchers and other standards-setting organizations are followed for the design and conduct of sample surveys. A technical report is produced for every survey which describes the sampling plan, the problems encountered in the field and the methods of resolution, and these are being improved to allow computation of margins of error that include design effects where feasible.

FY 2014 Performance Objectives and Outcomes

The BBG Agency-level performance objectives and measures are further supported and linked to language service and support service performance plans that have action steps and detailed performance goals and measures. Listed below are the BBG annual performance objectives, including key initiatives supported by the FY 2013 and 2014 enhancements, with summaries of the current status. Detailed accomplishments by regional performance objectives are also presented in the accomplishments table in the following pages.

REACH THE ARABIC SPEAKING WORLD.

Increase audience reach in the Maghreb region with strategic newsgathering that speaks directly to its target audience.

MBN is establishing small bureaus in the Maghreb region to expand newsgathering from the region. Bureaus in Tunis and Rabat will open in 2014.

Integrate Radio Free Iraq into MBN's Radio Sawa to reduce duplication.

Due to the deteriorating security situation in Iraq, BBG is maintaining all broadcasting to Iraq, including Radio Free Iraq and Radio Sawa.

EXPAND AUDIENCE REACH IN STRATEGIC LOCATIONS IN THE NEAR EAST, SOUTH, CENTRAL ASIA AND EURASIA

Focus broadcasting on formats and platforms that audiences favor.

VOA explored and implemented changes in radio programming in order to free up modest staff resources for use in expanding and enhancing television and digital/social media products that are increasingly preferred by audiences in target markets, including Russia, Georgia, and Pakistan.

Leverage the newsgathering assets of VOA and RFE/RL and increase coordination in countries where both entities broadcast.

VOA explored and implemented changes in radio programming in order to free up modest staff resources for use in expanding and enhancing television and digital/social media products that are increasingly preferred by audiences in target language services, including Russian, Georgian, Kurdish, and Urdu.

FOCUS BROADCASTING TO AUDIENCES OF STRATEGIC PRIORITY IN EAST ASIA.

Reach new audiences through satellite television in Burma.

VOA Burmese expanded production of its 30-minute television news program to go live seven days a week with placement on a national channel.

Leverage the newsgathering assets of VOA and RFA and increase coordination in countries where both entities broadcast.

BBG launched a joint 24/7 satellite stream to China featuring VOA and RFA content in four languages – Mandarin, Cantonese, Tibetan and Uyghur.

TARGET AFRICAN BROADCASTING TO AREAS PRONE TO TERROR INCIDENTS, GENOCIDE, OR FAILED STATES.

Counter the growing threat of extremism in the Trans-Sahel region of Africa through a multi-channel information and engagement campaign for youth.

VOA Hausa launched Dandalin VOA, a dynamic 24/7 Hausa-language news and information stream designed specifically for mobile devices with youth-oriented music programming, peak-hour news blocks, and short mobile-friendly feature segments.

Increase engagement with African audiences through reporting on local news and other relevant issues, including health, business, and technology.

VOA began new broadcasts for audiences in Central African Republic, South Sudan, and Mali.

EXPAND AUDIENCE REACH IN STRATEGIC LOCATIONS OF LATIN AMERICA.

Expand reach and impact in Latin America by serving as a U.S. Bureau and global news provider for affiliates throughout the region.

VOA continued to provide value for affiliates in Latin America with locally-relevant news and information, including coverage of unrest in Venezuela and unaccompanied minors from Central America crossing the U.S. border.

Increase newsgathering and production collaborating between VOA Spanish and OCB, freeing resources in both organizations to better serve their respective audiences with unique content that reflects the missions of each organization.

OCB and VOA Spanish continued to work cooperatively, sharing space and technical services, exchanging story information, and airing each other's programs where appropriate.

ALIGN ESSENTIAL SUPPORT FUNCTIONS WITH BROADCASTING IMPLEMENTATION STRATEGIES AND PERFORMANCE GOALS.

Realign BBG transmissions to maximize the effectiveness of program delivery resources.

During FY 2014, BBG took steps to reduce less effective legacy distribution systems, such as shortwave transmission, toward use of more modern technologies, where appropriate, to reach growing and younger audience.

Provide cutting-edge circumvention tools to audiences in countries that restrict and censor Internet access.

In FY 2014, the Internet Anti-Censorship (IAC) team countered online censorship in 13 countries and supported 21 BBG language services.

Increase awareness of BBG programs in high priority markets through advertising and promotion.

The BBG, through the Office of Strategy and Development, ensured that marketing efforts were aligned with high priority markets.

Use research to identify appropriate target audiences and their preferred media, with the formats and content that would appeal to them.

Comprehensive audience research and analysis was available to BBG language services and managers for planning and measuring performance.

Maintain the firewall and continuously monitor programming quality in line with modern broadcast

journalism principles through annual performance reviews of all broadcast services.

Annual program reviews were conducted by each broadcast entity with all rated broadcasting services receiving "good or better" program quality scores. No firewall violations were reported.

Support initiatives to improve financial, performance, and budget integration as well as improve financial and acquisition processes.

BBG continued to improve integration of financial and procurement management. IBB is leading a comprehensive reform of agency acquisitions to streamline process and reduce administrative burdens.

Carry out BBG's mission and goals with a workforce that is agile, skilled, diverse, well-led, and motivated.

IBB created a new structure for contract workers, in response to contractor feedback, and continued to implement the workplace engagement action plan, addressing challenges identified in the annual employee survey.

Address BBG's most critical infrastructure maintenance and repair requests.

The Office of Technology, Services, and Innovation addressed critical infrastructure issues including office space consolidation, realignment of transmission assets, and migration from satellite to fiber delivery.

Summary of FY 2014 Performance Accomplishments

FY 2014 Performance Objective

REACH THE ARABIC SPEAKING WORLD
WEEKLY AUDIENCE: 29.3 MILLION

FY 2014 Accomplishments

COVERING THE UNITED STATES

Alhurra and Radio Sawa ensured that the United States and its policies were accurately presented to the people of the Middle East. MBN has full-time correspondents covering the White House, Congress, the Pentagon and the State Department with reports and coverage of key statements, speeches, and hearings featured daily. For example, as part of Alhurra's coverage of Iraq's battle against the ISIS insurgency, the network aired President Obama's June 13 remarks, live with simultaneous translation into Arabic; Alhurra-Iraq was the only Arabic language channel to carry the briefing live.

ELECTION COVERAGE IN MIDDLE EAST

As voters went to the polls in Iraq, Egypt, Tunisia, and Algeria, Alhurra and Radio Sawa provided context for the people striving to effect greater economic, civil, and political stability. Alhurra and Radio Sawa provided balanced, unique insight through coverage of the Egyptian Constitutional Referendum and Presidential Elections, Iraqi Parliamentary Elections, Algerian Presidential Election and Afghan Presidential Election.

CRISIS REPORTING

Alhurra and Radio Sawa continued to report from Gaza and Israel with reporters on the front lines, as well as reaction from the White House, State Department, and Congress.

Since sectarian violence began to escalate in Iraq, Alhurra-Iraq and Radio Sawa continued to provide a balanced source of news and information with live updates from hotspots including Kirkuk, Irbil and just outside the city of Mosul in Kalak. The Syrian civil war and the Syrian refugee crisis were covered daily by Alhurra and Radio Sawa. Alhurra regularly carried United Nations briefings regarding relief efforts in Syria and the UN's renewed investigation into war crimes in Syria.

COMPELLING CONTENT

Alhurra continued its commitment to develop original content from the region, connecting with its viewers at the street level, through original, non-scripted programs like *Rayheen ala Fain* (*Where do we go from here?*) and *Street Pulse*. The critically acclaimed *Rayheen ala Fain* launched its second season with an entirely new cast of six Egyptian young adults. Episodes tackled very difficult social issues such as sexual harassment, the rights of women, jobs, and education.

Top: Alhurra correspondent Yehia Qassem reporting from Israel near Gaza. Bottom Left: Alhurra's *Rayheen ala Fain? (Where Are We Going?)* follows the day-to-day lives of May, Heba, Moheb, Sarah, Ahmed and Mamdouh as they respond to the daily challenges facing all Egyptians. Alhurra cover's the 2014 Iraq Elections.

FY 2014 Performance Objective

EXPAND AUDIENCE REACH IN STRATEGIC LOCATIONS IN THE NEAR EAST, SOUTH, CENTRAL ASIA AND EURASIA WEEKLY AUDIENCE: 59.1 MILLION

FY 2014 Accomplishments

INCREASED BROADCASTING TO UKRAINE
In response to events in Ukraine, VOA and RFE/RL ramped up Ukrainian coverage and added new programs. VOA Ukrainian is the go-to source for U.S. reaction and perspective on the crisis for top national television channels in Ukraine. According to a BBG-commissioned national survey of Ukraine in late April, one in five adults now consume BBG content weekly (20.8 percent). RFE/RL's Ukrainian Service provided dynamic coverage of the evolving situation in Ukraine, maintaining a live video stream, live-blogging coverage, and providing in-depth analysis of unfolding events. Innovative use of live streaming technologies to report from the scene of events resulted in the unprecedented growth of RFE/RL's Ukrainian Service website: 60 million visits and 112 million page views in the first half of 2014 – a tenfold increase over the same period in 2013.

COUNTERING RUSSIAN DISINFORMATION
To counter Kremlin influence in the Russian-language media space, RFE/RL and VOA expanded programming to the Russian periphery. At RFE/RL, new Russian-language programs are being produced by the Central Asian Services jointly, the Kyrgyz Service, and the Moldovan Service. In May 2014, VOA Ukrainian launched *Studio Washington*, a daily Russian-language television newscast aimed at curtailing a pro-Kremlin disinformation campaign and focusing on the U.S. and Western response to Moscow's aggression against Ukraine. VOA's Russian Service offered a targeted mix of digital and TV programming that provided an accurate portrayal of America, explained its policies and institutions, and addressed distortions and misperceptions about the U.S. and its policies.

In May, VOA Ukrainian launched *Studio Washington*, a daily Russian-language television newscast aimed at countering pro-Kremlin disinformation.

HARMONIZING CONTENT AND PROGRAMMING

Throughout FY 2014, VOA and RFE/RL worked closely to harmonize the content and program streams of their common language services. In January, RFE/RL's Azerbaijani Service began running three of VOA's Azerbaijani Service programs on its Azatliqradiosu TV satellite stream on Hotbird. In April 2014, RFE/RL's Georgian Service (Radio Tavisupleba) ramped up its radio programming to 18 hours daily via FM affiliate Radio Green Wave, including content from RFE/RL's Georgian Service, Ekho Kavkaza (Russian language to Georgia) unit, Russian Service, Armenian Service and Azerbaijani Service, as well as VOA's Georgian Service, Special English Service and Music Mix. In July 2014, RFE/RL's Armenian Service began harmonizing web content with VOA's Armenian Service.

ELECTION COVERAGE IN AFGHANISTAN

RFE/RL's Radio Free Afghanistan joined with state broadcaster RTA to sponsor two presidential candidate debates in Kabul in February. Eight of the 11 registered candidates took part in the debates with an RFE/RL moderator. VOA provided wall-to-wall coverage of the June 14 presidential runoff election in Afghanistan, including an exclusive interview with outgoing President Hamid Karzai.

REACHING AUDIENCES IN IRAN

VOA television programs to Iran are watched weekly by 24 percent of the adult population, making VOA Persian the leading international broadcaster in Iran. Radio Farda's incisive coverage on the web and social media helped the Service reach significant new audiences in 2013 and 2014, with the number of "likes" on Facebook nearing 1.2 million.

RFE/RL's Radio Free Afghanistan partnered with state broadcaster RTA to bring the Afghan people two presidential debates moderated by Akbar Ayazi RFE/RL's Regional Director for Afghanistan and Pakistan.

FY 2014 Performance Objective

FOCUS BROADCASTING TO AUDIENCES OF STRATEGIC PRIORITY IN EAST ASIA | WEEKLY AUDIENCE: 47.1 MILLION

FY 2014 Accomplishments

HONG KONG PROTESTS

RFA and VOA provided news and information on the protests in Hong Kong for audiences in mainland China, despite media blackouts, with a multi-platform strategy that includes shortwave, satellite, and digital. They have seen an increase in audience engagement with user-generated content, first-person observations, and expert analysis.

24/7 SATELLITE STREAM

BBG launched a joint 24/7 satellite stream to China featuring VOA and RFA content in four languages – Mandarin, Cantonese, Tibetan and Uyghur. The stream is also available for live streaming online.

CRISIS RESPONSE BROADCASTING TO THAILAND

When the Thai military suspended radio and TV broadcasts in May, VOA Thai started a daily, live 30-minute satellite radio-on-TV and webcast, and ramped up its efforts on Facebook, YouTube and Twitter. Engaged users on Facebook soared from the usual 2,000 per week to more than 25,000 per week during the crisis.

REPORTING ON ETHNIC MINORITIES

RFA's Uyghur Service was at the forefront of breaking news from inside China's Xinjiang Uyghur Autonomous Region (XUAR). RFA's Cantonese and Mandarin Services also enhanced coverage of ethnic unrest in the XUAR, reporting on the failure of Beijing's policies toward national minorities.

VOA Wei Shi, a daily program on BBG's 24/7 satellite stream, goes beyond the latest headlines with live reports from VOA correspondents in China and around the world including in the United States, London, Hong Kong, Taiwan, Moscow and Tokyo.

INCREASED REPORTING IN MYANMAR

VOA established an official news bureau in Yangon, Myanmar in January 2014, posting its first full-time Burmese correspondent there in May. VOA its 30-minute television news program to go live seven days a week with placement on a national channel.

PRESS CITATIONS IN NORTH KOREA

South Korea's TV Chosun channel reported that the North Korean Workers' Party newspaper – circulated only among senior party members – had cited VOA Korean reports more than any other foreign news media.

INVESTIGATIVE REPORT ON SAFETY OF NUCLEAR POWER PLANT IN CHINA

Despite increased security measures across China in anticipation of the 25th anniversary of the Tiananmen Square massacre, RFA's Cantonese Service concluded a six-month undercover investigation into operational safety in nuclear power plants in Guangdong, China's most populous province. A two-part multimedia report based on the findings of the investigation will air in FY 2015.

ENGAGING IN SOCIAL MEDIA IN CAMBODIA

VOA Khmer's Facebook page reached 500,000 fans in March 2014 – a 10-fold increase in a little more than a year, making it the second largest Khmer-language page on the site.

FOCUS ON WATER ISSUES

RFA launched a major social media campaign to educate audiences on the problem of clean water. As reports of deteriorating quality and quantity of fresh water supplies continue to come in, RFA is now positioned as one of the authoritative news sources on the topic internationally.

Radio Free Asia's Water Project is a multimedia project combining investigative and citizen journalism to focus on the state of freshwater and its availability in RFA broadcast countries

FY 2014 Performance Objective

TARGET AFRICAN BROADCASTING TO AREAS PRONE TO TERROR INCIDENTS, GENOCIDE, OR FAILED STATES WEEKLY AUDIENCE: 51.0 MILLION

FY 2014 Accomplishments

EBOLA COVERAGE

VOA English, French and Hausa produced hundreds of stories and informational products related to Ebola since the outbreak was first reported in March. Ebola related content is woven through regular radio and television programs, call-in shows, special reports, targeted mobile and web sites and social media campaigns. For example, VOA Hausa launched an Ebola Digital Awareness Campaign to help raise awareness in Nigeria and Hausa-speaking West Africa on how to prevent contracting and spreading the disease.

COVERING NIGERIA AND BOKO HARAM

VOA Hausa provided ground-breaking journalism with coverage of the terrorist insurgency in and around Nigeria. This year, a VOA Hausa reporter spent four weeks traveling through some of the most dangerous areas in Nigeria, the epicenter of Boko Haram. He provided multimedia coverage of major stories, including the abduction of more than 200 school girls by Boko Haram. During the past year, VOA Hausa has become the single most popular service in VOA's digital portfolio, averaging over four million visits per month. It launched *Dandalin VOA*, a dynamic 24/7 Hausa-language news and information stream designed specifically for mobile devices with youth-oriented music programming, peak-hour news blocks, and short mobile-friendly feature segments.

VOA Hausa created an in-depth multimedia investigative report on Boko Haram in Nigeria.

CENTRAL AFRICAN REPUBLIC

Responding to the crisis in the Central African Republic (CAR), this past year, VOA launched two 10-minute daily broadcasts in Sango on its FM station in the capital, Bangui. VOA French to Africa also broadcasts on the stream, adding local content in five daily news breaks during morning drive hours.

INCREASED COVERAGE IN SOUTH SUDAN

When civil strife broke out in South Sudan, VOA increased its broadcasting to the target region, adding 10 new on-the-spot reporters in strife-torn locations around the country. VOA developed and launched a targeted FM radio stream in Juba that carries news about South Sudan, interactive daily segments on a variety of topics, public service announcements, and other specialized news and entertainment.

LARGE WEEKLY REACH IN SOMALIA

VOA Somali continued to be a reliable source of information in the troubled Horn of Africa region, where over 40 percent of adults cite VOA as one of their leading sources of information, and more than half the population (51 percent) listens to VOA weekly.

NEW PROGRAM FOR MALI

A year after launching its first-ever Bambara language radio show for audiences in Mali, VOA added a new call-in program, *Anba Fo* (*We'll Say It*). The hour-long weekly radio show airs Saturday evenings on VOA's owned-and-operated FM station in Bamako, as well as online. Each episode addresses a topic critical to audiences in Mali, such as security and stability, education, women's rights and youth unemployment. Partnership with Leading Independent Nigerian Television Affiliate.

Given the rise of insurgency and civil conflict in Africa, VOA established a partnership with a leading independent Nigerian television station, enabling VOA's English to Africa Service to circumvent the Nigerian government's ban on international broadcasters. This means that VOA correspondents can file live reports on one of Nigeria's most popular private broadcasters, reaching approximately a 15 percent audience share of adults over age 15.

VOA Somali's 15-minute weekly TV show *Qubanaha* is available to audiences in Somalia and diaspora communities around the world.

FY 2014 Performance Objective

EXPAND AUDIENCE REACH IN STRATEGIC LOCATIONS IN LATIN AMERICA | WEEKLY AUDIENCE: 28.3 MILLION

FY 2014 Accomplishments

ON THE GROUND COVERAGE IN CUBA
During the past two years, OCB has doubled the number of news reports it produces in Cuba. The Martís have assembled the largest network of independent journalists working inside Cuba. These journalists file reports (which include audio, text, video, and photos) from across Cuba via telephone, SMS, and Internet.

SUPPORTING AFFILIATES IN VENEZUELA WITH CONTENT AND ANTI-CENSORSHIP TOOLS
Since February, when protesters in Venezuela were met with violent resistance by government forces, audiences have come to rely on VOA reports that air on TV affiliates throughout the region for accurate and balanced accounts of the protests and the government's response. VOA supports its affiliates, beyond just providing content; it has teamed with Radio Free Asia to provide affiliates with Internet circumvention tools to counter government efforts to crack down on independent media and influential social networks.

EMPOWERING CUBANS TO USE NEW MEDIA WITHOUT CENSORSHIP
In May, OCB launched *Reporta Cuba*, a new effort of the Martís to empower Cubans to communicate and engage in new media. *Reporta Cuba* is a network of citizen reporters – students, independent journalists, activists, dissidents, and regular citizens – who share information with OCB via SMS, MMS, and email from their mobile phones and computers. *Reporta Cuba* helps Cubans use available tools to disseminate information and report what they experience, without censorship.

COVERAGE OF THE BORDER CRISIS
VOA affiliates throughout Latin America relied daily on VOA Spanish Service's wall-to-wall coverage of the crisis over the unaccompanied minors from Central America crossing the U.S. border.

VOA Spanish has provided on-going in-depth coverage of the border crisis.

FY 2014 Performance Objective

ALIGN ESSENTIAL SUPPORT FUNCTIONS WITH BROADCASTING IMPLEMENTATION STRATEGIES AND PERFORMANCE GOALS.

FY 2014 Accomplishments

COUNTERING CENSORSHIP ON THE INTERNET

The BBG's Internet Anti-Censorship (IAC) team countered Internet censorship in 13 countries and supported 21 BBG language services. The team continued the expanded use of a mobile application for Android devices that incorporates a social news reader, social reporter to accept user-generated content, and real-time chat functionality targeted at users in Iran.

MOVING TO A MORE COST EFFICIENT AND FLEXIBLE GLOBAL DELIVERY NETWORK

In order to reduce telecommunications costs and move toward a more flexible and advanced global delivery data network, TSI completed the first phase of the Agency migration from expensive, dedicated transoceanic satellite and fiber circuits to the more flexible and less expensive digital Multi-Protocol Label Switching (MPLS) circuits. TSI successfully connected two major BBG distribution hubs located in the Philippines and Germany to the Agency's global MPLS network.

INTERNATIONAL JOURNALIST TRAINING

The Office of Strategy and Development promoted press freedom and built capacity among media by training hundreds of journalists in South Sudan, Nigeria, Ivory Coast, Burundi, Tanzania, DRC, Uganda, South Africa, Indonesia, Jamaica, and Bangladesh, among others. Training topics included political reporting, ethics, best practices in journalism, health, education, entrepreneurship, environment, and use of new technologies. OSD worked with reporters, editors and news managers to encourage professionalism and an understanding of the vital role of media in democracy.

NEW DIGITAL DELIVERY PLATFORM FOR AFFILIATES

The ODDI Digital Services team worked closely with the OSD Marketing team to develop a new platform for the BBG's global affiliates and digital partners around the world. The new BBG Direct features video and audio content from all five broadcast entities and offers affiliates a streamlined and cost-effective way to receive broadcast-quality USIM programming to distribute on-air and online to local audiences.

COMPREHENSIVE REFORM OF AGENCY ACQUISTIONS

The IBB is leading a comprehensive reform of agency acquisitions. In collaboration with VOA, staff in the Director's Office and the Office of Contracts issued a solicitation that will create a new structure for acquiring contract staff to support VOA and OCB programming. This new structure will streamline the administrative processes required for these contractors and significantly reduce the administrative burden for a significant portion of the agency's workforce.

Use of Performance Data to Promote Improved Outcomes

The BBG undertakes quantitative, qualitative, evaluative, and ad hoc research projects every year to directly support decisions on programming and strategy. Since FY 2002, the BBG has used a consolidated contract to procure audience and market research for all BBG broadcast services. The Agency maintains a vast database of audience and market data that consolidates research results. The archive covers some 100 countries and contains socioeconomic and demographic data as well as strategically important information on local media, competition, and audience preferences and needs. The research guides BBG strategic planning at all levels, specifically on-air program development, program reviews, and the Agency's comprehensive annual strategic review of all language services.

LANGUAGE SERVICE REVIEW

The Annual Language Service Review (LSR) is a Board directed, comprehensive assessment of the languages in which the BBG entities broadcast. The process fulfills the Congressional mandate in the U.S. International Broadcasting Act of 1994 to "review, evaluate, and determine, at least annually, after consultation with the Secretary of State, the addition or deletion of language services."

BBG analyzes data in key areas that shape priorities, including press freedom, political freedom, civil liberties, economic freedom and human development indices from nongovernmental organizations (e.g., Freedom House, The Heritage Foundation and The Wall Street Journal, and the United Nations Development Programme). These indicators are combined into a prioritization index that enables BBG to evaluate changing conditions worldwide.

This year's LSR considered additional inputs. First, the State Department's regional bureaus provided prioritization of BBG language services relative to U.S. foreign policy, as well as additional priority languages that BBG should consider for broadcast. Second, in response to a GAO review of overlap in BBG operations, the Agency developed a detailed matrix of content, cost, personnel, facilities, research and other information on every USIM language service as well as on other international and commercial broadcasters operating in the same languages.

STRATEGY REVIEW

In FY 2014, BBG completed its first comprehensive Strategy Review that considered how the Agency's mission is carried out by the networks in each target country and region. BBG language services presented their highest priority goals for the coming year in a series of regional meetings. This was an iterative process that considered input from language services, network management, IBB, and selected parties in the interagency, particularly the State Department.

The results of the Strategy Review include summaries of the political context, media environments, target audiences, foreign policy elements, and BBG objectives in each country and region. It also includes goals based on the strategic plan and performance targets for each BBG target area for FY 2015. Language and support services will be measured on progress toward these goals and targets, giving BBG an opportunity to define success, monitor performance and take corrective actions when goals are not met.

PROGRAM REVIEW

Each BBG entity conducts yearly reviews of each of its language services and their programming in order to maintain high quality broadcasts and to help the language services progress toward their strategic goals. These reviews are scheduled to include fresh research data and analysis about the media market and audiences in the area that each program targets. Survey data allow both for the development of future strategies in response to media trends, as well as a review of the services' performance across key indicators, such as the size and positive experience of the audience. Program Reviews further analyze the quality of news and information programming by examining a sample of broadcast material, editorial controls and supervision, utilizing monitoring panels, and tracking regular audiences' perceptions of the trustworthiness and reliability of the entity's news and information.

After the Program Review, program quality scores are assigned to the language services. Historically, this measure has combined scores of external monitoring panels with the analysis of in-house analysts. During the transition to a new research provider, the BBG is evaluating and restructuring how it conducts external quality analysis. Scores for FY 2012 through 2014 are based exclusively on in-house ratings. Program review analysts facilitate the development of an action plan with each service and the support elements to improve program quality and/or delivery, and to move the service toward completion of its strategic goals.

Independent Program Evaluations

The BBG conducts several types of annual independent evaluations to assess effectiveness and strategic priorities. The annual Language Service Review conducted by the Board assesses the question of where the BBG should broadcast, fulfilling the congressional mandate to "review, evaluate, and determine, at least annually, after consultation with the Secretary of State, the addition and deletion of language services." A new Strategy Review process was implemented in FY 2014, which identified target audiences and set country-level goals for each of BBG's markets. Program Reviews, conducted for the individual language services, will assess progress against these goals, as well as serve as annual quality control mechanisms based on field research and expert analysis. Taken together, these review processes are a significant source of information and analysis used for managing the BBG.

- The Office of the Inspector General (OIG) provides the BBG and Congress with systematic and independent evaluations of the operations of the BBG, designed to prevent and detect waste, fraud, and abuse, including: whether resources are being used and managed with maximum efficiency; whether financial transactions and accounts are properly conducted, maintained, and reported; whether the administration of activities and operations meets the requirements of applicable laws and regulations; whether internal management

controls have been instituted to ensure quality of performance and reduce the likelihood of mismanagement; and whether adequate steps for detection, correction, and prevention have been taken.

- OIG inspections also generally review whether policy goals and objectives are being effectively achieved. However, Public Law 103-236 states that the OIG "shall respect the journalistic integrity of all the broadcasters and may not evaluate the philosophical or political perspectives reflected in the content of broadcasts."

- The Government Accountability Office (GAO) audits Agency operations to determine whether federal funds are being spent efficiently and effectively, including investigating allegations of illegal and improper activities, reporting on how well government programs and policies are meeting their objectives, and performing policy analyses and outlining options for Congressional consideration. GAO also advises Congress and the heads of executive agencies about ways to make government more efficient, effective, ethical, equitable, and responsive.

The BBG maintains a productive relationship with the OIG and GAO. The BBG works to ensure that the inspections, audits, and reviews produce reports that are based on relevant facts with an understanding of the programs and operations involved. The resulting recommendations assist the Agency in improving administration and management of its programs and operations.

During FY 2014, the OIG issued ten final reports for BBG; the GAO did not issue any reports about BBG. The Agency will continue to implement and respond to the recommendations of these evaluations.

OIG reports issued in FY 2014 are summarized below.

OIG AUDIT OF THE BROADCASTING BOARD OF GOVERNORS INFORMATION SECURITY PROGRAM

Through an external audit firm, the OIG conducted the annual evaluation of BBG's Information Security Program, in accordance with the Federal Information Security Management Act of 2002. The audit found that BBG made progress in FY 2013 in security awareness training and account management, but significant challenges remain. BBG needs to address several control weaknesses in areas including:

risk management framework, continuous monitoring program, enterprise-wide and system-specific contingency plan, incident response and reporting program, and the Plans of Action and Milestones process. The report contains thirteen recommendations, all of which the BBG concurred with and is working to implement.

OIG AUDIT OF BROADCASTING BOARD OF GOVERNORS FY 2013 COMPLIANCE WITH IMPROPER PAYMENTS REQUIREMENTS

The OIG conducted this third annual audit to assess BBG's FY 2012 compliance with IPIA, as amended by IPERA. The OIG found that BBG was in substantial compliance with improper payments requirements. Specifically, BBG had conducted an improper payments risk assessment of its significant programs and reported the required improper payments information in its FY 2013 Performance

and Accountability Report (PAR). However, the OIG found that BBG's improper payments risk assessment identified high improper payment error rates and that BBG did not notify OMB and OIG of its decision not to perform payment recapture audits. The OIG issued two recommendations, both of which have now been resolved.

INSPECTION OF EMBASSY ABU DHABI AND CONSULATE GENERAL DUBAI, UNITED ARAB EMIRATES

The OIG inspection of the Consulate General Dubai included a review of MBN's production center. No recommendations were issued related to BBG operations.

OIG AUDIT OF THE BROADCASTING BOARD OF GOVERNORS ADMINISTRATION AND OVERSIGHT OF ACQUISITION FUNCTIONS

The OIG conducted an audit of BBG's acquisition functions to evaluate whether BBG had adequate acquisition policies and procedures and to assess the efficacy of those policies and procedures. The OIG notified BBG that it had reportable violations of the Anti-Deficiency Act. The OIG found a number of additional areas in which BBG had not complied with Federal regulations related to procurement.

The OIG made two principal recommendations: develop an action plan with measurable goals and milestones and develop and implement enforcement mechanisms to assist in ensuring enhanced accountability for compliance with procurement regulations. In addition, the OIG issued 36 other recommendations.

OIG REPORT ON FY 2013 RISK ASSESSMENT OF TRAVEL AND PURCHASE CARD PROGRAMS AT THE BROADCASTING BOARD OF GOVERNORS

The OIG conducted an assessment of agency purchase and travel card programs and identified and analyzed associated risks. The OIG found that the risk of illegal, improper, or erroneous use in BBG's travel card program was "medium" and in the purchase card

program "very low." These risk levels do not require annual audits, but the OIG suggests that travel and purchase card program managers take appropriate actions to ensure and improve oversight of the programs.

INSPECTION OF EMBASSY BUJUMBURA, BURUNDI

The OIG inspection of Embassy Bujumbura included a review of BBG activities in Burundi. No recommendations were issued related to BBG operations.

INSPECTION OF EMBASSY KAMPALA, UGANDA

The OIG inspection of Embassy Kampala included a review of BBG marketing activities in Uganda. No recommendations were issued related to BBG operations.

OIG INSPECTION OF THE OFFICE OF CUBA BROADCASTING

The OIG conducted an inspection of the Office of Cuba Broadcasting (OCB). The OIG found that OCB is successfully implementing the agency Strategic Plan, as well as its own programming goals. They made 19 recommendations in areas including: contracting, performance evaluations, financial management, property management, records management, and security.

INSPECTION OF EMBASSY KABUL, AFGHANISTAN

The OIG inspection of Embassy Kabul included a review of the relationship between the embassy and VOA Afghan and RFE/RL Radio Free Afghanistan. No recommendations were issued related to BBG operations.

OIG AUDIT OF RADIO FREE EUROPE/RADIO LIBERTY AFTER-EMPLOYMENT BENEFITS

The OIG contracted an external firm to audit Radio Free Europe/Radio Liberty's (RFE/RL) after-employment benefits program. The audit firm found that RFE/RL had an unfunded liability associated with the program and insufficient monitoring on the part of BBG. The OIG made ten recommendations to improve BBG's oversight of RFE/RL's financial operations.

Section 3: Financial Information

Letter from the Chief Financial Officer 82

Independent Auditor's Report 84

Response to the Audit 100

Balance Sheet 101

Statement of Net Cost 102

Statement of Changes in Net Position 103

Statement of Budgetary Resources 104

Notes to Principal Financial Statements..................................... 106

Required Supplementary Information 126

Message from the Chief Financial Officer

I am honored to present the Fiscal Year (FY) 2014 financial statements for the Broadcasting Board of Governors (BBG). BBG is firmly committed to delivering the highest standard of financial accountability and reporting in support of the Agency mission of informing, engaging and connecting people around the world in support of freedom and democracy. This Performance and Accountability Report (PAR) is our principal report to the President, Congress and the American people on our stewardship of the public funds to which we have been entrusted and the great work by the agency to further our worldwide mission.

BBG received an unmodified audit opinion on its FY 2014 and FY 2013 financial statements. We worked diligently to address the material weaknesses identified by the auditors. Although there is additional work to be done, BBG believes we have made great strides in improving our position and addressing the issues. BBG increased our communication with the grantees to strengthen our understanding of their financial processes, funding reporting status and disposition. Through this increased understanding, BBG developed a revised methodology to account for and report the status of grantee advances. BBG is committed to continuing the effort and re-establishing the grantee monitoring program in FY 2015. In the area of property management, we have modified existing property policy and implemented process changes to ensure accurate recording and increased monitoring of agency assets. We plan to continue our commitment to strengthen our asset management efforts by recruiting a dedicated property manager. Additionally, in the area of lease accountability, we have changed our process to separately code these contracts to ensure the complete lease population is identified and analyzed for a capital lease determination. In the area of budgetary accounting and funds control, additional process controls were implemented on the financial reporting process to ensure accurate and complete financial reporting. For obligation monitoring, a dedicated budget analyst was assigned in FY 2014. A revised funds management policy and agencywide initiative will be implemented in FY 2015.

We are working diligently to meet the growing reporting, audit and compliance changes and requirements of OMB, Treasury and Congress. The Agency successfully met the new Treasury reporting requirements for our funds position through the Central Accounting Reporting System (CARS). In November we will be reporting our agency trial balance data through the Government-wide Treasury Account Symbol (GTAS) system. Our Improper Payments Elimination and Recovery Act results continue to show full compliance in the review and payment of domestic and internal payments. In FY 2015, the BBG will be implementing an Internal Control program in accordance with OMB A-123, Federal Managers Financial Integrity Act.

The BBG fully recognizes the importance and seriousness of the items noted in the PAR. Through the dedicated work of our staff, we are pleased with the successes in the current year and fully acknowledge there is additional work to be done in the coming year. We are confident through our continued committed efforts, and working in partnership with the independent financial auditors and the Office of Inspector General, we will successfully address and remediate the areas of concern.

André Mendes

Director of Global Operations

Acting Chief Financial Officer

November 17, 2014

Independent Auditor's Report

November 17, 2014

The Honorable Jeffrey Shell
Chair, Broadcasting Board
 of Governors
330 Independence Ave., SW, Room 3360
Washington, DC 20237

Dear Mr. Shell:

An independent certified public accounting firm, Kearney & Company, P.C., was engaged to audit the consolidated financial statements of the Broadcasting Board of Governors (BBG) as of September 30, 2014 and 2013, and for the years then ended; to provide a report on internal control over financial reporting; and to report any reportable noncompliance with laws, regulations, contracts, and grant agreements it tested. The contract required that the audit be performed in accordance with U.S. generally accepted government auditing standards and Office of Management and Budget audit guidance. In its *Independent Auditor's Report on the Broadcasting Board of Governors 2014 and 2013 Financial Statements* (AUD-FM-IB-15-10), Kearney & Company found

- the consolidated financial statements present fairly, in all material respects, the financial position of BBG as of September 30, 2014 and 2013, and its net cost of operations, changes in net position, and budgetary resources for the years then ended, in conformity with accounting principles generally accepted in the United States of America;

- three material weaknesses[1] in internal control over financial reporting; and

- instances of reportable noncompliance with laws, regulations, contracts, and grant agreements tested.

Kearney & Company is responsible for the enclosed auditor's report, which includes the Independent Auditor's Report, the Report on Internal Control Over Financial Reporting, and the Report on Compliance With Applicable Provisions of Laws, Regulations, Contracts, and Grant Agreements, dated November 12, 2014, and the conclusions expressed in the report. The Office

---

[1] A material weakness is a deficiency, or combination of deficiencies, in internal control, such that there is a reasonable possibility that a material misstatement of the entity's financial statements will not be prevented, or detected and corrected, on a timely basis.

U.S. Department of State, Office of Inspector General, Washington, D.C. 20522-0308

of Inspector General (OIG) does not express an opinion on BBG's consolidated financial statements or conclusions on internal control over financial reporting and compliance with laws, regulations, contracts, and grant agreements.

BBG's comments on the auditor's report are attached to the report.

OIG appreciates the cooperation extended to it and Kearney & Company by BBG managers and staff during this audit.

Sincerely,

Steve A. Linick
Inspector General

Enclosure: As stated.

cc: IBB – André Mendes

2

1701 Duke Street, Suite 500, Alexandria, VA 22314
PH: 703.931.5600, FX: 703.931.3655, www.kearneyco.com

INDEPENDENT AUDITOR'S REPORT
AUD-FM-IB-15-10

To the Board of Governors and the Inspector General of the Broadcasting Board of Governors

Report on the Financial Statements

We have audited the accompanying consolidated financial statements of the Broadcasting Board of Governors (BBG), which comprise the consolidated balance sheets as of September 30, 2014 and 2013, the related consolidated statements of net cost and changes in net position, and the combined statements of budgetary resources for the year then ended, and the related notes to the consolidated financial statements (hereinafter referred to as the "consolidated financial statements").

Management's Responsibility for the Financial Statements

Management is responsible for the preparation and fair presentation of these consolidated financial statements in accordance with accounting principles generally accepted in the United States of America; this includes the design, implementation, and maintenance of internal control relevant to the preparation and fair presentation of consolidated financial statements that are free from material misstatement, whether due to fraud or error.

Auditor's Responsibility

Our responsibility is to express an opinion on these consolidated financial statements based on our audits. We conducted our audits in accordance with auditing standards generally accepted in the United States of America; the standards applicable to financial audits contained in *Government Auditing Standards*, issued by the Comptroller General of the United States; and Office of Management and Budget (OMB) Bulletin No. 14-02, *Audit Requirements for Federal Financial Statements*. Those standards and OMB Bulletin No. 14-02 require that we plan and perform the audit to obtain reasonable assurance about whether the consolidated financial statements are free from material misstatement.

An audit involves performing procedures to obtain audit evidence about the amounts and disclosures in the financial statements. The procedures selected depend on the auditor's judgment, including the assessment of the risks of material misstatement of the financial statements, whether due to fraud or error. In making those risk assessments, the auditor considers internal control relevant to the entity's preparation and fair presentation of the financial statements in order to design audit procedures that are appropriate under the circumstances but not for the purpose of expressing an opinion on the effectiveness of the entity's internal control. Accordingly, we express no such opinion. An audit also includes evaluating the appropriateness of accounting policies used and the reasonableness of significant accounting estimates made by management, as well as evaluating the overall presentation of the financial statements.

1

We believe that the audit evidence we have obtained is sufficient and appropriate to provide a basis for our audit opinion.

Opinion on the Consolidated Financial Statements

In our opinion, the consolidated financial statements referred to above present fairly, in all material respects, the financial position of BBG as of September 30, 2014 and 2013, and its net cost of operations, changes in net position, and budgetary resources for the year then ended, in accordance with accounting principles generally accepted in the United States of America.

Other Matters

Required Supplementary Information

Accounting principles generally accepted in the United States of America require that the Management's Discussion and Analysis and Deferred Maintenance (hereinafter referred to as "required supplementary information") be presented to supplement the consolidated financial statements. Such information, although not a part of the consolidated financial statements, is required by OMB Circular A-136, *Financial Reporting Requirements*, and the Federal Accounting Standards Advisory Board, which consider it to be an essential part of financial reporting for placing the consolidated financial statements in an appropriate operational, economic, or historical context. We have applied certain limited procedures to the required supplementary information in accordance with auditing standards generally accepted in the United States of America, which consisted of inquiries of management about the methods of preparing the information and comparing it for consistency with management's responses to our inquiries, the consolidated financial statements, and other knowledge we obtained during our audits of the consolidated financial statements. We do not express an opinion or provide any assurance on the information because the limited procedures do not provide us with sufficient evidence to express an opinion or provide any assurance.

Other Information

Our audit was conducted for the purpose of forming an opinion on the consolidated financial statements as a whole. The information in the Message from the BBG Chairman, the Performance Information and the Other Information sections, as listed in the Table of Contents of BBG's *Performance and Accountability Report,* are presented for purposes of additional analysis and are not a required part of the consolidated financial statements. Such information has not been subjected to the auditing procedures applied in the audit of the consolidated financial statements, and accordingly, we do not express an opinion or provide any assurance on it.

Other Reporting Required by *Government Auditing Standards*

In accordance with *Government Auditing Standards* and OMB Bulletin No. 14-02, we have also issued reports, dated November 12, 2014, on our consideration of BBG's internal control over

2

financial reporting and on our tests of BBG's compliance with certain provisions of laws, regulations, contracts, and grant agreements for the year ended September 30, 2014. The purpose of those reports is to describe the scope of our testing of internal control over financial reporting and compliance and the results of that testing and not to provide an opinion on internal control over financial reporting or on compliance. Those reports are an integral part of an audit performed in accordance with auditing standards generally accepted in the United States of America, *Government Auditing Standards,* and OMB Bulletin No. 14-02, in considering BBG's internal control over financial reporting and compliance.

Kearney & Company

Alexandria, Virginia
November 12, 2014

3

1701 Duke Street, Suite 500, Alexandria, VA 22314
PH: 703.931.5600, FX: 703.931.3655, www.kearneyco.com

INDEPENDENT AUDITOR'S REPORT ON INTERNAL CONTROL OVER FINANCIAL REPORTING

To the Board of Governors and the Inspector General of the Broadcasting Board of Governors

We have audited the consolidated financial statements of the Broadcasting Board of Governors (BBG) as of and for the year ended September 30, 2014, and have issued our report thereon dated November 12, 2014. We conducted our audit in accordance with auditing standards generally accepted in the United States of America; the standards applicable to financial audits contained in *Government Auditing Standards*, issued by the Comptroller General of the United States; and Office of Management and Budget (OMB) Bulletin No. 14-02, *Audit Requirements for Federal Financial Statements*.

Internal Control Over Financial Reporting

In planning and performing our audit of the consolidated financial statements, we considered BBG's internal control over financial reporting (internal control) as a basis for designing audit procedures that are appropriate under the circumstances for the purpose of expressing our opinion on the consolidated financial statements but not for the purpose of expressing an opinion on the effectiveness of BBG's internal control. Accordingly, we do not express an opinion on the effectiveness of BBG's internal control. We limited our internal control testing to those controls necessary to achieve the objectives described in OMB Bulletin No. 14-02. We did not test all internal controls relevant to operating objectives as broadly defined by the Federal Managers' Financial Integrity Act of 1982, such as those controls relevant to ensuring efficient operations.

Our consideration of internal control was for the limited purpose described in the preceding paragraph and was not designed to identify all deficiencies in internal control that might be material weaknesses or significant deficiencies; therefore, material weaknesses or significant deficiencies may exist that were not identified. However, as described in the following sections, we identified certain deficiencies in internal control that we consider to be material weaknesses and significant deficiencies.

A deficiency in internal control exists when the design or operation of a control does not allow management or employees, in the normal course of performing their assigned functions, to prevent, or detect and correct, misstatements on a timely basis. A material weakness is a deficiency, or combination of deficiencies, in internal control, such that there is a reasonable possibility that a material misstatement of the entity's financial statements will not be prevented, or detected and corrected, on a timely basis. We consider the following deficiencies in BBG's internal control to be material weaknesses.

1

Material Weaknesses

I.   Grantee Monitoring and Accounting for Grant Advances

BBG has three grantees that it funds through annual grant agreements: Radio Free Europe/Radio Liberty, Radio Free Asia, and the Middle East Broadcasting Networks. The grantees are responsible for developing broadcast content (radio and television news programs), which is distributed by BBG. The three grantees annually receive approximately $245 million, one third of BBG's total funding. In our FY 2013 Independent Auditor's Report on Internal Control Over Financial Reporting, we identified control deficiencies relating to BBG's management of its grantees that, when combined, constituted a material weakness in internal control. During FY 2014, BBG's control environment continued to exhibit deficiencies that negatively impacted BBG's ability to effectively monitor its grantees and report grant advances. We concluded that the combination of these deficiencies was a material weakness. The individual deficiencies we identified are summarized as follows:

- Grantee Monitoring – BBG is responsible for monitoring how its grantees use BBG funds to ensure the grantees adhere to relevant laws and regulations as well as the terms and conditions specified in the grant agreements. During the FY 2013 financial statement audit, we found that BBG did not sufficiently monitor its three grantees. For example, BBG had not obtained inventory listings for all grantees, did not ensure grantees had required procurement procedures, and did not assess grantee expenditures to ensure that the expenditures were allowable under the terms of the grant agreement. In FY 2014, BBG management communicated that there had not been significant improvements to the grantee monitoring process.

  BBG was assessing potential corrective actions that would bring its grantee monitoring into compliance with Federal regulations; however, these actions had not been executed. For example, BBG had not improved its grantee handbook to define roles and responsibilities for responsible officials. BBG had also not developed tools, templates, or best practices to ensure procedures were being appropriately executed. Further, BBG had not developed a process to ensure oversight activities were communicated between different officials involved in the oversight process. BBG officials stated that limited resources and competing priorities impacted their ability to implement planned corrective actions. BBG officials stated that they anticipated that BBG would be able to implement grantee monitoring procedures in FY 2015. A lack of effective grantee oversight increases the risk of waste, fraud, and abuse of Federal funds.

- Grant Advances – Funds that BBG provides to its grantees that have not been expended by the grantees are considered grant advances. We analyzed BBG's grant advance estimation methodology and identified flaws in the methodology and underlying assumptions that had not been fully validated. The methodology was based primarily on funding requests submitted by the grantees to BBG and expenses reported on the grantee's trial balances. We found that BBG

2

- Excluded funds provided to grantees prior to FY 2008.
- Did not identify and exclude grantee funds that were provided by third parties from its advance estimate.
- Miscalculated certain grantee expenses in its estimation methodology. For example, BBG's grant advance calculations did not consider the impact of the grantees' year-end accounting entries.

BBG's methodology to estimate grant advances was flawed because BBG officials did not have a sufficient understanding of grantee financial reporting practices and lacked internal quality control procedures over accrual calculation. In addition, we noted that BBG did not perform sufficient procedures to confirm the reasonableness of the estimate. Without a sufficient understanding of its grantees' financial reporting processes, BBG may continue to base its grants advance estimate on inappropriate assumptions, which could negatively impact BBG's ability to monitor grantee funding requirements.

II. Property, Plant, and Equipment

As of September 30, 2014, BBG reported over $115 million in net property, plant, and equipment (PP&E), which included real and personal property. In our FY 2013 audit, we identified control deficiencies with BBG's PP&E processes that, when combined, constituted a material weakness in internal control. During our FY 2014 audit, we continued to identify deficiencies that limited BBG's ability to report PP&E in a complete and accurate manner. We concluded that the combination of these deficiencies was a material weakness. The individual deficiencies we identified are summarized as follows:

- Property Records – BBG owns personal property, such as vehicles and other tangible items valued at $25,000 or more, located at domestic and overseas locations. BBG uses an internally developed system, the Property Inventory Processing System (PIPS), to track property. The data in PIPS are used to calculate the property balances reported in BBG's financial statements. To ensure that personal property was properly recorded as assets, we performed a series of tests that identified several exceptions. Specifically, we

  - Judgmentally selected a sample of 42 assets during site visits to domestic BBG locations and found 27 assets (64 percent) that were not recorded in PIPS.
  - Analyzed expense transactions related to security equipment purchases and identified six items of security equipment that were not recorded in PIPS.
  - Performed analytical procedures for two large overseas locations and found that BBG had purchased and improperly recorded three pieces of equipment as expenses rather than assets at one of the locations.

BBG does not have current, comprehensive, and clear policies or procedures to ensure that property is effectively managed and reported. We also found that BBG has not clearly defined roles and responsibilities related to the property management process. Not all employees, such as procurement and receiving officials, had a clear understanding of their role in the process. In addition, BBG lacks centralized oversight and monitoring procedures to ensure accountability and accurate reporting across the organization.

3

Although BBG had a process in place to periodically assess expenditures to identify potential unrecorded capital assets, this process was insufficient because it did not assess transactions recorded using certain codes. BBG also did not have an effective process to ensure that property inventories were appropriately performed and reported. Two of the locations where we performed testing had not performed physical inventories during FY 2014 as required. We also identified flaws in the physical inventory process. For example, the physical inventory process did not include procedures to ensure the completeness of property records, such as tracing assets physically observed during inventory procedures back to the respective site's PIPS property records.

The lack of appropriate property management procedures and controls results in the loss of accountability over assets, which could lead to undetected waste or theft. In addition, incomplete or inaccurate property records result in misstatements of BBG's financial statements.

- Property Removed From Service – Agencies are responsible for ensuring that PP&E is appropriately valued and reported in the financial statements. Assets that are no longer providing service to the organization should be written off and should not be included in the financial statements. We identified 16 assets included in BBG's financial statements that were impaired, obsolete, or permanently removed from service. The assets were located at two BBG transmitting facilities that had ceased operations in 2007 and were permanently out of service. We also identified these 16 items as retired assets during our audit of BBG's FY 2013 financial statements. BBG removed them from the FY 2013 financial statements.

  To address the FY 2013 financial statement audit finding, BBG financial reporting officials obtained additional information from property officials on the items removed from service. Because of a misinterpretation of the information provided, the financial reporting officials recorded the items at an incorrect value. Although BBG's financial reporting staff performs reconciliations and analyses prior to reporting its PP&E balances, they were not fully knowledgeable about the standards for recording assets permanently identified as inactive. As a result, PP&E was misstated.

III. Budgetary Accounting and Funds Control

Budgetary accounting refers to the processes, controls, monitoring, and reporting required to track the execution of budget laws. In our FY 2013 audit, we identified control deficiencies related to budgetary accounting that, when combined, constituted a material weakness in internal control. In FY 2014, BBG continued to lack sufficient reliable funds control to ensure budgetary transactions were properly recorded, monitored, and reported. We concluded that the combination of control deficiencies remained a material weakness. The individual deficiencies we identified are summarized as follows:

- Unliquidated Obligations – BBG should record an obligation in its financial management system when it enters into an agreement, such as a contract or a purchase order, to

4

purchase goods and services. Once recorded, obligations remain open until they are fully reduced by disbursements, are deobligated, or until the appropriation funding the obligations is cancelled. Unliquidated obligations (ULO) represent the cumulative amount of orders, contracts, and other binding agreements for which the goods and services ordered have not been received or the goods and services have been received but payment has not yet been made. BBG reported more than $127 million in ULOs as of September 30, 2014.

To assess the validity of ULOs, we tested a sample of 124 ULOs and found 68 invalid ULOs (55 percent). For domestic obligations, BBG had not effectively implemented and formalized ULO review policies and procedures. Specifically, BBG officials did not perform timely follow-up with program offices to ensure invalid domestic ULOs were identified and liquidated. Without formal policy guidance from BBG, the Budget Office's efforts to monitor obligation validity may not be considered a priority for the Program Offices. Further, BBG did not conduct a review of overseas ULOs to confirm validity. As a result of the identified errors, BBG significantly overstated its obligations. These funds could have been used for other purposes but remained unnecessary obligations.

- Timeliness of Obligations – We identified a number of instances where obligations were not created in a timely manner, such as obligations that were not recorded within 15 days of executing obligating document, obligations that were recorded prior to executing the obligating document, and obligations that were posted subsequent to the receipt of goods and services or the start of the period of performance for a contract. BBG did not have an adequate process in place to ensure that its employees were complying with Federal requirements related to the creation, approval, and timely recording of obligations. Without an effective obligation process, controls to monitor funds and make timely payments may be compromised, which may lead to violations of the Antideficiency Act and the Prompt Payment Act.

- Apportioned Authority – Prior to using appropriated funds, the funds must be apportioned to BBG by OMB. Apportionment authority allows OMB to regulate the rate of fund usage by agencies. We found that BBG incorrectly reported certain transactions in the draft Statement of Budgetary Resources as unapportioned authority rather than as apportioned authority. BBG did not have a process to reconcile and confirm apportionment records from OMB to the information reported in the Statement of Budgetary Resources. If BBG does not have a process to reconcile and confirm its apportioned authority, its financial statements may be misstated.

A significant deficiency is a deficiency, or combination of deficiencies, in internal control that is less severe than a material weakness yet important enough to merit attention by those charged with governance. We consider the following deficiency in BBG's internal control to be a significant deficiency.

5

Significant Deficiency

I.   Information Technology

BBG uses several financial management systems to compile information for financial reporting purposes. BBG's main domestic financial management and accounting system is Momentum, which is provided by an external service provider. The external service provider is responsible for maintaining a number of information technology (IT) controls. However, Momentum is accessed through BBG's general IT support system. Therefore, IT deficiencies noted in the general support system could potentially impact Momentum as well. For overseas accounting and budget execution, BBG uses the Regional Financial Management System (RFMS) provided by the Department of State (Department). The Department is responsible for maintaining an adequate general and application control environment over this system.

The Office of Inspector General (OIG) annually performs an evaluation of BBG and Department information security program compliance with IT provisions as required by the Federal Information Security Management Act (FISMA).

In FY 2013, we and OIG noted control structure limitations surrounding the general support system and financial management applications used by BBG, which we considered to be a significant deficiency. Although BBG and the Department had remediated deficiencies related to financial management applications used by BBG in FY 2014, OIG continued to identify weaknesses and vulnerabilities in the general support system maintained by BBG and the Department. When combined, we considered the control deficiencies impacting the general support system to be a significant deficiency.

Collectively, the control deficiencies noted by OIG in its FY 2014 FISMA report[1] related to BBG's general support system represented a significant deficiency to enterprise-wide security as defined by OMB guidance. OIG reported that the most significant security deficiencies were related to BBG's risk management framework, continuous monitoring program, and the incident response and reporting program. These control weaknesses impacted BBG's general support system, which is used to access the Momentum system.

OIG's FY 2014 FISMA report[2] for the Department identified deficiencies with the general support system at the Department similar to the deficiencies identified at BBG. OIG concluded that the issues identified were a significant deficiency to enterprise-wide security. RFMS is hosted on the Department's general support system.

In general, OIG found that BBG had not implemented effective standards, policies, processes, and procedures over its information security program. For RFMS, because of the deficiencies noted with the IT security program at the Department, BBG needs to implement additional controls to ensure that financial information is being processed accurately and completely by the Department.

---

[1] *Audit of the Broadcasting Board of Governors Information Security Program* (AUD-IT-IB-15-13, Oct. 2014).
[2] *Audit of Department of State Information Security Program* (AUD-IT-15-17, Nov. 2014).

6

Poor controls over IT security can affect the integrity of financial applications, which increases the risk that sensitive financial information could be accessed by unauthorized individuals or that financial transactions could be altered either accidentally or intentionally. IT weaknesses increase the risk that BBG will be unable to report financial data accurately.

During the audit, we noted certain additional matters involving internal control over financial reporting that we will report to BBG management in a separate letter.

Status of Prior Year Findings

In the Independent Auditor's Report on Internal Control Over Financial Reporting included in the audit report on BBG's 2013 financial statements,[3] we noted several issues that were related to internal control over financial reporting. The status of these issues is summarized in Table 1.

Table 1. Status of Prior Year Findings

Control Deficiency	FY 2013 Status	FY 2014 Status
Grantee Monitoring and Accounting for Grant Advances	Material Weakness	Material Weakness
Property, Plant, and Equipment	Material Weakness	Material Weakness
Budgetary Accounting and Funds Control	Material Weakness	Material Weakness
Information Technology	Significant Deficiency	Significant Deficiency

BBG's Response to Findings

BBG management has provided its response to our findings in a separate letter attached to this report. We did not audit management's response, and accordingly, we express no opinion on it.

---

[3] *Independent Auditor's Report on the Broadcasting Board of Governors 2013 Financial Statements* (AUD-FM-IB-14-14, Dec. 2013).

7

Purpose of This Report

The purpose of this report is solely to describe the scope of our testing of internal control over financial reporting and the results of that testing and not to provide an opinion on the effectiveness of BBG's internal control. This report is an integral part of an audit performed in accordance with auditing standards generally accepted in the United States of America, *Government Auditing Standards*, and OMB Bulletin No. 14-02 in considering BBG's internal control over financial reporting. Accordingly, this report is not suitable for any other purpose.

Kearney & Company

Alexandria, Virginia
November 12, 2014

8

1701 Duke Street, Suite 500, Alexandria, VA 22314
PH: 703.931.5600, FX: 703.931.3655, www.kearneyco.com

INDEPENDENT AUDITOR'S REPORT ON COMPLIANCE WITH APPLICABLE PROVISIONS OF LAWS, REGULATIONS, CONTRACTS, AND GRANT AGREEMENTS

To the Board of Governors and the Inspector General of the Broadcasting Board of Governors

We have audited the consolidated financial statements of the Broadcasting Board of Governors (BBG) as of and for the year ended September 30, 2014, and have issued our report thereon dated November 12, 2014. We conducted our audit in accordance with auditing standards generally accepted in the United States of America; the standards applicable to financial audits contained in *Government Auditing Standards*, issued by the Comptroller General of the United States; and Office of Management and Budget (OMB) Bulletin No. 14-02, *Audit Requirements for Federal Financial Statements*.

Compliance

As part of obtaining reasonable assurance about whether BBG's consolidated financial statements are free from material misstatement, we performed tests of its compliance with certain provisions of laws, regulations, contracts, and grant agreements, noncompliance with which could have a direct and material impact on the determination of financial statement amounts, and certain provisions of other laws and regulations specified in OMB Bulletin No. 14-02 that we determined were applicable. We limited our tests of compliance to these provisions and did not test compliance with all laws, regulations, contracts, and grant agreements applicable to BBG. However, providing an opinion on compliance with those provisions was not an objective of our audit, and accordingly, we do not express such an opinion.

The results of our tests disclosed instances of noncompliance that are required to be reported under *Government Auditing Standards* and OMB Bulletin No. 14-02 and which are summarized as follows:

- *Federal Grant Regulations*. BBG is responsible for monitoring the use of funds provided to its grantees to ensure the grantees adhere to relevant laws and regulations. During the audit of BBG's FY 2013 financial statements, we identified substantial noncompliance with Federal grant regulations. As noted in our Independent Auditor's Report on Internal Control Over Financial Reporting, BBG was assessing potential corrective actions to bring its grantee monitoring into compliance with Federal regulations, but these actions had not been executed in FY 2014. As a result, BBG continued to be in substantial noncompliance with the following Federal grant regulations:

  - OMB Circular A-110, *Uniform Administrative Requirements for Grants and Agreements With Institutions of Higher Education, Hospitals, and Other Non-Profit Organizations*, sets forth standards for obtaining consistency and uniformity among Federal agencies in the administration of grants to non-profit organizations.

1

- OMB Circular A-122, *Cost Principles for Non-Profit Organizations*, establishes principles for determining the costs of grants, contracts, and other agreements with non-profit organizations.
- OMB Circular A-133, *Audits of States, Local Governments, and Non-Profit Organizations*, sets forth standards for obtaining consistency and uniformity among Federal agencies for the audit of non-profit organizations expending Federal awards.

- *Prompt Payment Act.* This act requires Federal agencies to make payments in a timely manner and to pay interest penalties when payments are late. BBG did not always make payments within 30 days, as required. Additionally BBG did not always pay interest on payments made after the 30-day requirement or accurately calculate the interest that was paid.

- *Federal Acquisition Regulation.* The Federal Acquisition Regulation is the primary guidance for Federal acquisitions of supplies and services using appropriated funds. In FY 2013, the Office of Inspector General conducted an audit of BBG's administration and oversight of acquisition functions[4] and identified instances of noncompliance with the Federal Acquisition Regulation. During our audit of the FY 2014 financial statements, BBG officials indicated that although BBG had begun to develop corrective action plans, many of the deficiencies identified by the Office of Inspector General remained unaddressed, resulting in acquisition processes and activities that were not compliant with Federal procurement regulations.

- *Federal Managers' Financial Integrity Act* – The Federal Managers' Financial Integrity Act requires executive branch agencies to establish and maintain effective internal control. The heads of agencies must annually evaluate and report on the effectiveness of the internal control and financial management systems that protect the integrity of Federal programs. We found that BBG did not complete its annual evaluation in FY 2014.

During the audit, we noted certain additional matters involving compliance that we will report to BBG management in a separate letter.

BBG's Response to Findings

BBG management has provided its response to our findings in a separate letter attached to this report. We did not audit management's response, and accordingly, we express no opinion on it.

---

[4] *Audit of the Broadcasting Board of Governors Administration and Oversight of Acquisition Functions* (AUD-CG-IB-14-26, June 2014).

2

Purpose of This Report

The purpose of this report is solely to describe the scope of our testing of compliance and the results of that testing and not to provide an opinion on the effectiveness of BBG's compliance. This report is an integral part of an audit performed in accordance with auditing standards generally accepted in the United States of America, *Government Auditing Standards*, and OMB Bulletin No. 14-02, in considering BBG's compliance. Accordingly, this report is not suitable for any other purpose.

Kearney & Company

Alexandria, Virginia
November 12, 2014

3

Response to the Audit

BROADCASTING BOARD OF GOVERNORS
UNITED STATES OF AMERICA

November 17, 2014

The Honorable Steve A. Linick
Deputy Inspector General
Office of Inspector General
U.S. Department of State

Dear Mr. Linick:

The Performance and Accountability Report (PAR) is our principal report to the President, Congress and the American taxpayer, shedding light on our stewardship of the public funds with which we have been entrusted. It is a key vehicle for sharing the BBG's financial status in full transparency and establishing the concomitant levels of accountability.

The PAR provides a comprehensive account of the BBG's financial activities in the context of our global mission in fulfilling the charter of the organization as part of the United States public diplomacy apparatus.

I am pleased to report that the BBG has received an unqualified opinion for this fiscal year's financial audit. While we recognize that there were three material weaknesses and one significant deficiency identified that will require continued attention and an increased focus going forward, we remain committed to ensuring that the significant progress registered in several areas during this past year will be further augmented this year and in the future. Our commitment to regulatory compliance, financial management, and sound internal controls will be a key portion of our management's performance measures as we address the identified issues.

Our goal is to achieve maximum compliance, transparency and accountability as we continue to operate a truly complex global operation working in some of the most challenging environments in the world. We continue to excel in our mission to inform, engage and connect people around the world in support of freedom and democracy while remaining seriously challenged by the rapid transformation of media markets, continuingly increasing operational portfolios and dwindling financial resources.

In the midst of these challenges, we are confident that the BBG will continually improve the quality of its operations while it expands its global reach in the fulfillment of the United States International Media goals.

We would be remiss if we did not thank Kearney & Company for their sustained efforts and professionalism in working through the many complex issues associated with the global nature of BBG's financial processes.

Sincerely,

André V. Mendes
Acting Chief Financial Officer

330 INDEPENDENCE AVENUE, SW   ROOM 3360   COHEN BUILDING   WASHINGTON, DC 20237   (202) 203-4545   FAX (202) 203-4568

Broadcasting Board of Governors
Consolidated Balance Sheet
As of September 30, 2014 and 2013
(in thousands)

	FY 2014	FY 2013
Assets (Note 2):		
Intragovernmental:		
Fund Balance with Treasury (Note 3)	$ 191,082	$ 161,420
Accounts Receivable, Net (Note 4)	22	102
Total Intragovernmental	191,104	161,522
Accounts Receivable, Net (Note 4)	204	10
Advances to Surrogate Broadcasters (Note 5)	55,000	45,576
General Property, Plant and Equipment, Net (Note 6)	116,411	118,407
Other (Note 7)	6,324	10,982
Total Assets	$ 369,043	$ 336,497
Liabilities (Note 8):		
Intragovernmental:		
Accounts Payable	$ -	$ -
Accrued FECA Liability (Note 8)	1,603	1,689
Other (Note 11)	2,144	1,381
Total Intragovernmental	3,747	3,070
Accounts Payable	28,986	28,915
Actuarial FECA Liabilities (Note 8)	7,167	7,233
Accrued Payroll and Benefits	6,947	5,435
Foreign Service Nationals After-Employment Benefits (Note 8 and 9)	8,554	4,444
Environmental and Disposal Liabilities (Note 8 and 10)	1,079	1,061
Accrued Annual and Compensatory Leave (Note 8)	16,442	16,864
Contingent Liabilities (Note 8 and 13)	9,760	6,288
Other (Note 11)	69	1,170
Total Liabilities	$ 82,751	$ 74,480
Net position:		
Unexpended Appropriations	$ 196,694	$ 162,659
Cumulative Results of Operations	89,598	99,358
Total Net Position	$ 286,292	$ 262,017
Total Liabilities and Net Position	$ 369,043	$ 336,497

Broadcasting Board of Governors
Consolidated Statement of Net Cost
For the Years Ended September 30, 2014 and 2013
(in thousands)

	FY 2014	FY 2013
Voice of America		
Gross Costs (Note 14)	$ 348,649	$ 370,575
Less: Earned Revenues	(3,426)	(3,646)
Net Program Costs	345,223	366,929
Office of Cuba Broadcasting (OCB) - Radio and TV Marti		
Gross Costs (Note 14)	49,435	45,770
Less: Earned Revenues	-	-
Net Program Costs	49,435	45,770
Surrogate Broadcasters		
Gross Costs (Note 14)	330,747	327,010
Less: Earned Revenues	-	-
Net Program Costs	330,747	327,010
Total Gross Costs	728,831	743,355
Less: Total Earned Revenues	(3,426)	(3,646)
Net Cost of Operations	$ 725,405	$ 739,709

The accompanying notes are an integral part of these statements.

Consolidated Statement of Changes in Net Position
For the Years Ended September 30, 2014 and 2013
(in thousands)

	All Other Funds	Consolidated Total	
	FY 2014	FY 2014	FY 2013
Cumulative Results of Operations:			
Beginning Balances	$ 99,358	$ 99,358	$ 100,417
Adjustments:			
Correction of Errors	-	-	-
Beginning Balance, as Adjusted	99,358	99,358	100,417
Budgetary Financing Sources:			
Other Adjustments	-	-	-
Appropriations Used	699,595	699,595	719,572
Non-Exchange Revenue	-	-	-
Other	53	53	36
Other Financing Sources (Non-Exchange):			
Donated Revenue-Nonfinancial Resources	-	-	1
Transfers In/Out Reimbursement	1,220	1,220	-
Imputed Financing	14,791	14,791	19,063
Other	(14)	(14)	(22)
Total Financing Sources	715,645	715,645	738,650
Net Cost of Operations	(725,405)	(725,405)	(739,709)
Net Change	(9,760)	(9,760)	(1,059)
Cumulative Results Of Operations	89,598	89,598	99,358
Unexpended Appropriations:			
Beginning Balance	162,659	162,659	176,831
Adjustments:			
Beginning Balance as Adjusted	162,659	162,659	176,831
Budgetary Financing Sources:			
Appropriations Received	733,480	733,480	751,530
Appropriations Transferred In/Out	1,500	1,500	-
Other Adjustments	(1,350)	(1,350)	(46,130)
Appropriations Used	(699,595)	(699,595)	(719,572)
Total Budgetary Financing Sources	34,035	34,035	(14,172)
Total Unexpended Appropriations	196,694	196,694	162,659
Net Position	$ 286,292	$ 286,292	$ 262,017

The accompanying notes are an integral part of these statements.

Broadcasting Board of Governors
Combined Statement of Budgetary Resources
For the Years Ended September 30, 2014 and 2013
(in thousands)

	FY 2014	FY 2013
Budgetary Resources:		
Unobligated balance, brought forward, Oct 1	$ 46,776	$ 49,843
Adjustment to unobligated balance brought forward, Oct 1	-	(70)
Unobligated balance brought forward, Oct 1, as adjusted	46,776	49,773
Recoveries of prior year unpaid obligations	9,355	7,059
Other changes in unobligated balance	151	(8,085)
Unobligated balance from prior year budget authority, net:	56,282	48,747
Appropriations	733,948	713,954
Spending authority from offsetting collections:	6,341	8,105
Total budgetary resources	$ 796,571	$ 770,806
Status of Budgetary Resources:		
Obligations incurred:	$ 734,327	$ 724,030
Unobligated balance, end of year:		
Apportioned	28,286	12,514
Unapportioned	33,958	34,262
Total unobligated balance, end of year	62,244	46,776
Total budgetary resources	$ 796,571	$ 770,806

(Continues on next page)

Broadcasting Board of Governors
Combined Statement of Budgetary Resources
For the Years Ended September 30, 2014 and 2013
(in thousands) (Continued)

	FY 2014	FY 2013
Change in Obligated Balance		
Unpaid Obligations:		
Unpaid obligations brought forward, Oct 1	$ 122,849	$ 122,780
Adjustments to unpaid obligations, start of year		
Obligations incurred	734,327	724,030
Outlays, gross	(714,133)	(716,902)
Recoveries of prior year unpaid obligations	(9,355)	(7,059)
Unpaid obligations, end of year	133,688	122,849
Uncollected payments:		
Uncollected payments, federal sources, brought forward, Oct 1	(4,107)	(1,431)
Change in uncollected payments, federal sources	(1,728)	(2,676)
Uncollected payments, federal sources, end of year	(5,835)	(4,107)
Memorandum (non-add) entries:		
Obligated balance, start of year	$ 118,742	$ 121,349
Obligated balance, end of year	$ 127,853	$ 118,742
Budget Authority and Outlays, Net:		
Budget authority, gross	$ 740,289	$ 722,059
Actual offsetting collections	(4,613)	(5,429)
Change in uncollected customer payments from federal sources	(1,728)	(2,676)
Budget Authority, net	$ 733,948	$ 713,954
Outlays, gross	$ 714,133	$ 716,902
Actual offsetting collections	(4,613)	(5,429)
Outlays, net	709,520	711,473
Agency outlays, net	$ 709,520	$ 711,473

The accompanying notes are an integral part of these statements.

Broadcasting Board of Governors
Notes to Principal Financial Statements

For the Years Ended September 30, 2014 and 2013

NOTE 1: SUMMARY OF SIGNIFICANT ACCOUNTING POLICIES

A. Reporting Entity

On October 1, 1999, the Broadcasting Board of Governors (BBG) became the independent, autonomous entity responsible for all U.S. Government and government-sponsored, non-military, international broadcasting. This was the result of the 1998 Foreign Affairs Reform and Restructuring Act (Public Law 105-277). The federal agency is composed of four components:

- **Broadcasting Board of Governors (the Board)**
- **International Broadcasting Bureau (IBB)**
- **Voice of America (VOA)**
- **Office of Cuba Broadcasting (OCB)**

The Board and the IBB do not engage in the development of news content. The Board provides overall governance for the BBG and has authority to make grants to carry out its statutorily defined broadcasting mission. The IBB maintains the global distribution network over which all BBG-funded news and information programming is distributed. The IBB also provides administrative functions which are governed by federal laws and regulations. The VOA and OCB are the components of the agency that develop news content along with three surrogate broadcasters: Radio Free Europe/Radio Liberty (RFE/RL), Radio Free Asia (RFA), and the Middle East Broadcast Network (MBN). Every week, 215 million listeners, viewers, and Internet users around the world turn on, tune in, and log on to U.S. international broadcasting programs.

The surrogate broadcasters – RFE/RL, RFA, and MBN – are grantee organizations who receive the majority of their funding from the BBG. They are organized and managed as private, independent, not-for-profit corporations. Further information on these grantees can be found at:

- **Radio Free Europe/Radio Liberty – www.rferl.org**
- **Radio Free Asia – http://www.rfa.org/english**
- **Middle East Broadcasting Networks – www.alhurra.com**

B. Basis of Presentation and Accounting

These financial statements have been prepared to report the financial position, net cost, changes in net position, and budgetary resources of the BBG, consistent with the Chief Financial Officers' Act of 1990 and the Government Management Reform Act of 1994. These financial statements have been prepared from the books and records of the BBG in accordance with generally accepted accounting principles (GAAP) and Office of Management and Budget (OMB) Circular No. A-136, *Financial Reporting Requirements*. The GAAP for federal entities are the standards issued by the Federal Accounting Standards Advisory Board (FASAB) which is the designated standard-setting body for the Federal Government.

Financial transactions are recorded in the financial system, using both an accrual and a budgetary basis of accounting. Under the accrual method, revenues are recognized when earned, and expenses are recognized when a liability is incurred, without regard to the receipt or payment of cash. Budgetary accounting facilitates compliance with legal requirements and mandated controls over the use of federal funds. It generally differs from the accrual basis of accounting in that obligations are recognized when new orders are placed, contracts awarded, and services received that will require payments during the same or future periods.

C. Assets and Liabilities

Assets and liabilities presented on the BBG's balance sheets include both entity and non-entity balances. Entity assets are assets that the BBG has authority to use in its operations. Non-entity assets are held and managed by the BBG, but are not available for use in operations.

Intragovernmental assets and liabilities arise from transactions between the BBG and other federal entities. All other assets and liabilities result from activity with non-federal entities. Liabilities covered by budgetary or other resources are those liabilities of the BBG for which Congress has appropriated funds or funding is otherwise available to pay amounts due. Liabilities not covered by budgetary or other resources represent amounts owed in excess of available congressionally appropriated funds or other amounts. The liquidation of liabilities not covered by budgetary or other resources is dependent on future congressional appropriations or other funding.

D. Fund Balance with Treasury

Fund Balance with Treasury (FBWT) includes several types of funds available to pay current liabilities and finance authorized purchases.

General Funds

These consist of expenditure accounts used to record financial transactions arising from congressional appropriations, as well as receipt accounts.

Trust Funds

These are used for the acceptance and administration of funds contributed from public and private sources and programs.

Other Fund Types

These include miscellaneous receipt accounts, deposit and clearing accounts maintained to track receipts and disbursements awaiting proper classification.

The BBG does not maintain cash in commercial bank accounts for the funds reported in the balance sheet. Treasury processes domestic receipts and disbursements. Two Department of State financial service centers, located in Bangkok, Thailand and Charleston, South Carolina, provide financial support for the BBG operations overseas. The U.S. disbursing officer at each center has the delegated authority to disburse funds on behalf of the Treasury.

E. Accounts Receivable

Accounts receivable consists of amounts owed to the BBG by other federal agencies and the public. Intragovernmental accounts receivable represents amounts due from other federal agencies for reimbursable activities. Accounts receivable from the public represent amounts due from common carriers for unused airline tickets, and from vendors for erroneous or duplicate payments. These receivables are stated net of any allowances for estimated uncollectible amounts. The allowance, if any, is determined by the nature of the receivable and an analysis of aged receivable activity.

F. Advances and Prepayments

Payments made in advance of the receipt of goods and services are recorded as advances or prepayments, and recognized as expenses when the related goods and services are received. Advances are made principally to some BBG employees for official travel; salary advances to some BBG employees, often for employees transferring to overseas assignments; advance payments to other Federal entities as part of a reimbursable agreement; miscellaneous prepayments and advances to surrogate broadcasters for future services. Advances to surrogate broadcasters are described further in Note 5.

G. Personnel Compensation and Benefits

Annual, Sick and Other Leave Program

Annual leave and other leave time are accrued when earned, reduced when taken, and adjusted for changes in compensation rates. An unfunded liability is recognized for earned but unused annual leave as these balances will be funded from future appropriations in the year that leave is taken. Sick leave is expensed when taken, and no liability is recognized as employees are not vested in unused sick leave.

Retirement Plans

Civil Service employees participate in either the Civil Service Retirement System (CSRS) or the Federal Employees Retirement System (FERS). Employees covered under CSRS contribute 7 percent of their salary; the BBG contributes 7 percent. Employees covered under CSRS also contribute 1.45 percent of their salary to Medicare insurance; the BBG makes a matching contribution. On January 1, 1987, FERS went into effect pursuant to Public Law 99-335. Most employees hired after December 31, 1983, are automatically covered by FERS and Social Security. Employees hired prior to January 1, 1984, were allowed to join FERS or remain in CSRS. Employees participating in FERS contribute 0.80 percent of their salary, with the BBG making contributions of 11.9 percent. FERS employees also contribute 6.20 percent to Old Age Survivor and Disability Insurance (OASDI) and 1.45 percent to Medicare insurance. The BBG makes matching contributions to both. A primary feature of FERS is that it offers a Thrift Savings Plan (TSP) into which the BBG automatically contributes 1 percent of pay and matches employee contributions up to an additional 4 percent. CSRS-covered employees may make voluntary contributions to the TSP, but without the employer 1 percent contribution or employer-matching contributions. Effective January 1, 2013, pursuant to Public Law 112-96, Section 5001, new employees (as designated in the statute) will pay higher FERS employee contributions (3.1 percent instead of 0.80 percent) with BBG making contributions of 9.60 percent. These employees will be covered under the FERS as Revised Annuity Employees (RAE), FERS-RAE. Effective January 1, 2014, Section 401 of the "Bipartisan Budget Act of 2013," signed into law by the President on December 26, 2013, makes another change to the Federal Employees' Retirement System (FERS). New employees (as designated in the statute) will pay higher FERS employee contributions (4.4 percent instead of 0.80 percent) with BBG making contributions of 9.60 percent. These employees will be covered under the FERS as Further Revised Annuity Employees (FRAE), FERS-FRAE.

Note – FERS used here refers to the Federal Employees' Retirement System, the Foreign Service Pension System, and other equivalent Government retirement plans; CSRS used here includes the Civil Service Retirement System, CSRS Offset, the Foreign Service Retirement and Disability System, and other equivalent Government retirement plans.

Foreign Service employees participate in either the Foreign Service Retirement and Disability System (FSRDS) or the Foreign Service Pension System (FSPS). The FSRDS is the Foreign Service equivalent of CSRS as described in chapter 83 of Title 5, U.S.C. Employees covered under FSRDS contribute 7.25 percent of their salary; the BBG contributes 7.25 percent. Employees covered under FSRDS also contribute 1.45 percent of their salary to Medicare insurance; the BBG makes a matching contribution. The FSPS is the Foreign Service equivalent of the FERS, as described in chapter 84 of Title 5, U.S.C. In general, all Foreign Service eligible participants hired after December 31, 1983, participate in the FSPS. Most employees hired after December 31, 1983, are automatically covered by FSPS and Social Security. Employees hired prior to January 1, 1984, were allowed to join FSPS or remain in FSRDS. Employees participating in FSPS contribute 1.35 percent of their salary, with the BBG making contributions of 20.22 percent. FSPS employees also contribute 6.20 percent to OASDI and 1.45 percent to Medicare insurance. The BBG makes matching contributions to both. A primary feature of FSPS is that it offers a TSP into which the BBG automatically contributes 1 percent of pay and matches employee contributions up to an additional 4 percent. FSRDS-covered employees may make voluntary contributions to the TSP, but without the employer 1 percent contribution or employer-matching contributions. Effective January 1, 2013, pursuant to Public Law 112-96, Section 5001, new employees (as designated in the statute) will pay higher FSPS employee contributions (3.65 percent instead of 1.35 percent) with BBG making contributions of 17.92 percent. These employees will be covered under FSPS as Revised Annuity Employees (RAE), FSPS-RAE. The Department of State manages the FSRDS and FSPS plans.

Health Insurance

Most of the BBG's employees participate in the Federal Employees Health Benefits Program (FEHB), a voluntary program that provides protection for enrollees and eligible family members in case of illness, accident, or both. Under FEHB, the BBG contributes the employer's share of the premium as determined by the U.S. Office of Personnel Management (OPM).

Life Insurance

Unless specifically waived, employees are covered by the Federal Employees Group Life Insurance Program (FEGLI). FEGLI automatically covers eligible employees for basic life insurance in amounts equivalent to an employee's annual pay. Enrollees and their family members are eligible for additional insurance coverage, but the enrollee is responsible for the cost of the additional coverage. Under FEGLI, the BBG contributes the employer's share of the premium, as determined by OPM.

Workers' Compensation

The Federal Employees' Compensation Act (FECA) provides income and medical cost protection to covered federal civilian employees injured on the job, to employees who have incurred work-related occupational diseases, and to beneficiaries of employees whose deaths are attributable to job-related injuries or occupational diseases. The FECA program is administered by the U.S. Department of Labor (DOL), which initially pays valid claims and subsequently seeks reimbursement from federal agencies employing the claimants.

The FECA liability consists of two components. First is a current liability amount based on actual claims paid by DOL but not yet reimbursed by the BBG. Timing of the BBG's reimbursement to DOL is dependent on appropriated funds made available for this purpose and generally occurs two to three years after actual claims had been paid.

The second FECA component is the actuarial estimate of future benefit payments for death, disability, medical, and miscellaneous costs. This estimate is determined using a method that analyzes historical benefit payment patterns related to a specific period in order to predict the ultimate payments related to the current period. The estimated liability is not covered by budgetary resources and will require future funding.

Federal Employees Post-Employment Benefits

The BBG does not report CSRS, FERS, FEHB or FEGLI assets, accumulated plan benefits, or unfunded liabilities applicable to its employees; OPM reports this information. As required by Statements of Federal Financial Accounting Standards (SFFAS) No.5, Accounting for Liabilities of the Federal Government, the BBG reports the full cost of employee benefits for the programs that OPM administers. The BBG recognizes an expense and imputed financing source for the annualized unfunded portion of CSRS, post-retirement health benefits, and life insurance for employees covered by these programs. The additional costs are not actually owed or paid to OPM, and thus are not reported as liabilities on the balance sheet.

Foreign Service Nationals (FSN) After-Employment Benefits

The BBG employs approximately 300 FSN employees at 24 overseas posts. Many of these posts offer some type of after-employment benefits that are based on the employment laws and prevailing wage practices in that host country. These benefits include annuity-based defined benefit plans, defined contribution plans, and lump sum voluntary severance and retirement benefits. Descriptions of these after-employment benefits and projected plan benefits are presented in fuller details in Note 9.

H. Contingent Liabilities

Contingencies are accrued in the financial statements for claims where potential losses are probable and the cost is measurable. Cases for which the likelihood of an unfavorable outcome is less than probable but more than remote, the estimated range of loss is disclosed but not accrued, as presented in Note 13.

I. Revenues and Financing Sources

The BBG operations are financed through congressional appropriations, reimbursement for the provision of goods or services to other federal agencies, transfers and donations. Financing sources are received in direct annual and no-year appropriations; these appropriations may be used, within statutory limits, for operating and capital expenditures.

Work performed for other federal agencies under reimbursable agreements is initially financed through the account providing the service and is subsequently reimbursed. Reimbursements are recognized as revenue when earned, i.e., goods have been delivered or services rendered, and the associated costs have been incurred.

An imputed financing source is recognized to offset costs incurred by the BBG and funded by another federal source, in the period in which the cost was incurred. The types of costs offset by imputed financing are employees' pension benefits, health insurance, life insurance, and other post-retirement benefits for employees. Funding from other federal agencies is recorded as an imputed financing source.

J. Net Position

The BBG's net position contains the following components:

Unexpended Appropriations

This is the sum of undelivered orders and unobligated balances. Undelivered orders represent the amount of obligations incurred for goods or services ordered, but not yet received. An unobligated balance is the amount available after deducting cumulative obligations from total budgetary resources. As obligations for goods or services are incurred, the available balance is reduced.

Cumulative Results of Operations

These include (1) the accumulated difference between revenues and financing sources less expenses since inception; (2) the BBG's investment in capitalized assets financed by appropriation; (3) donations; and (4) unfunded liabilities, for which liquidation may require future congressional appropriations or other budgetary resources.

K. Management's Use of Estimates

The preparation of financial statements requires management to make estimates and assumptions affecting the reported amounts of assets, liabilities, revenues, expenses, and the disclosure of contingent liabilities. Actual results could differ from these estimates.

L. Statement of Net Cost Presentation

The presentation of the Statement of Net Cost is aligned by the two federal entities displayed separately and the three grantees, or surrogate broadcasters, displayed aggregately. Although there is one overarching goal in the Strategic Plan, this presentation reflects the reporting entity of federal and surrogate broadcasting components.

NOTE 2: ENTITY / NON-ENTITY ASSETS

Assets of the BBG include entity assets and non-entity assets. Non-entity assets are currently held by but not available to the BBG. They are restricted by nature and consist of amounts in deposit and miscellaneous receipts held for others. The funds will be forwarded to Treasury or other entities at a future date. Non-entity assets as of September 30, 2014 and 2013 are summarized as follows:

Entity / Non-Entity Assets (in thousands)	2014	2013
Intragovernmental		
Fund Balance with Treasury	$ 1,112	$ (2,747)
Accounts Receivable	15	6
Prepayments for Judgment Fund	-	3,846
Total Non-Entity Assets	1,127	1,105
Total Entity Assets	367,916	335,392
Total Assets	$ 369,043	$ 336,497

NOTE 3: FUND BALANCE WITH TREASURY

Treasury performs cash management activities for all federal agencies. The net activity represents Fund Balance with Treasury. The Fund Balance with Treasury represents the right of the BBG to draw down funds from Treasury for expenses and liabilities.

Fund Balance with Treasury by fund type as of September 30, 2014 and 2013, consists of the following:

Fund Balances (in thousands)	2014	2013
General Funds	$ 182,490	$ 158,190
Trust Funds	7,608	7,329
Other Fund Types	984	(4,099)
Total	$ 191,082	$ 161,420

The status of Fund Balance with Treasury as September 30, 2014 and 2013 consists of the following:

Status of Fund Balance with Treasury (in thousands)	2014	2013
Unobligated Balance		
Available	$ 31,146	$ 21,113
Unavailable	31,099	25,663
Obligated Balance Not Yet disbursed	127,853	118,743
Non-Budgetary Fund Balance with Treasury	984	(4,099)
Total	$ 191,082	$ 161,420

The status of the fund balance may be classified as unobligated available, unobligated unavailable, obligated balance not yet disbursed, and non-budgetary Fund Balance with Treasury. Unobligated available funds, depending on budget authority, are generally available for new obligations in the current fiscal year. The unobligated unavailable amounts are those appropriated in prior fiscal years but not available to fund new obligations; however they are available to increase existing prior year obligations. The obligated but not yet disbursed balance represents amounts designated for payment of goods and services ordered but not yet received, or goods and services received but for which payment has not yet been made.

Canceled funds returned to Treasury as September 30, 2014 and 2013, totaled $1.3 million and $8.1 million, respectively.

NOTE 4: ACCOUNTS RECEIVABLE, NET

Accounts receivable as of September 30, 2014 and 2013, are as follows:

Accounts Receivable (in thousands)	2014	2013
Intragovernmental	$ 22	$ 102
Public	219	19
Allowance for Uncollectable Accounts	(15)	(9)
Total Accounts Receivable, Net	**$ 226**	**$ 112**

NOTE 5: ADVANCES TO SURROGATE BROADCASTERS

The advance to surrogate broadcasters (or grantees) is an amount in which the BBG has disbursed funds but for which goods and services have not been delivered or performed. Grant funds are issued on an advance basis and liquidated based on actual expenses incurred by the grantee as of September 30, 2014. BBG is in the process of refining its grant advance liquidation methodology. The FY2014 grant advance liquidation approach utilized expenses as recorded in the grantee's unaudited Trial Balances through August 2014. Actual advance liquidations for the last period of the year are not known at the time financial statements are prepared. As a result, BBG accrues for grant expenses incurred but not reported. The FY2014 grant expense accrual applied an average of the percentage increase of expenses incurred in September over those incurred in August. In FY 2013, BBG's grant accrual methodology estimated expenses for the year and was based on the grantees' cash balances at year end less an average of the prior year's liabilities, as included on the grantee's audited A-133 financial statements.

Advances to surrogate broadcasters for the years ended September 30, 2014 and 2013 is $55 million and $45.6 million, respectively.

NOTE 6: PROPERTY, PLANT, AND EQUIPMENT, NET

Property, plant, and equipment consist of equipment, buildings, vehicles, and land. There are no restrictions on the use of property, plant, and equipment. The BBG capitalizes property, plant, and equipment with a useful life of two years or more. The thresholds for capitalization are as follows: equipment costing $25,000 or more, buildings and capital leases costing more than $100,000, and other structures and facilities costing $50,000 or more. In addition, ADP software costing over $250,000, and all land, land rights, and vehicles are capitalized, regardless of cost.

Expenditures for normal repairs and maintenance are expended unless the expenditure is equal to or greater than $25,000 and the improvement increases the asset's useful life by two years or more, in which case the amounts are capitalized.

Depreciation or amortization is computed using the straight-line methodology over the assets' useful lives ranging from five to thirty years. Amortization of capitalized software begins on the date it is put in service, if purchased, or when the module or component has been successfully tested if developed internally. Amortization of capital leases is over the term of the lease.

Property, plant, and equipment consist of property used in operations and consumed over time. The following table summarizes cost and accumulated depreciation/amortization of property, plant, and equipment as of September 30, 2014 and 2013.

PP&E *(in thousands)*		2014			2013		
Property Category	Useful Life (Years)	Cost	Accumulated Depreciation	Net Book Value	Cost	Accumulated Depreciation	Net Book Value
Land	N/A	$ 3,848	$ -	$ 3,848	$ 3,848	$ -	$ 3,848
Building	30	25,219	(17,441)	7,778	23,733	(16,555)	7,178
Other Structures	20	8,073	(6,754)	1,319	7,875	(6,559)	1,316
Construction-in-Progress	N/A	3,611	-	3,611	1,200	-	1,200
Equipment	6-30	314,675	(221,146)	93,529	313,180	(214,033)	99,147
Vehicles	6	5,662	(4,526)	1,136	5,946	(4,654)	1,292
Assets under Capital Lease	10	2,040	(2,040)	-	2,040	(2,040)	-
Leasehold Improvements	10	2,770	(127)	2,643	1,800	-	1,800
Software	5	4,747	(2,564)	2,183	4,747	(2,121)	2,626
Internal Use of Software in Development	N/A	364	-	364	-	-	-
Total		$ 371,009	$ (254,598)	$ 116,411	$ 364,369	$ (245,962)	$ 118,407

Depreciation and amortization expense as of September 30, 2014 and 2013 is $12.3 million and $13.1 million, respectively.

NOTE 7: OTHER ASSETS

Other assets consist of (a) general PP&E that is no longer in service and is awaiting disposal, retirement or removal from service, and is recorded at estimated net realizable value; and, (b) advances and prepayments to BBG employees for official travel, miscellaneous prepayments, and salary advances to BBG employees transferring to overseas assignments. Other assets consist of the following as of September 30, 2014 and 2013:

Other Assets (in thousands)	2014	2013
Inactive PP&E	$ 5,314	$ 5,634
Travel/Salary Advance	1,010	1,502
Prepayments for Judgment Fund	-	3,846
Total	**$ 6,324**	**$ 10,982**

NOTE 8: LIABILITIES NOT COVERED / COVERED BY BUDGETARY RESOURCES

The BBG's liabilities are classified as covered or not covered by budgetary resources. Liabilities not covered by budgetary resources are liabilities for which Congressional action is needed before budgetary resources can be provided. They include the annual leave, workers compensation, pensions and other retirement benefits, and certain environmental matters as described in Note 10 – Environmental and Disposal Liability.

Liabilities Covered / Not Covered by Budgetary Resources (in thousands)	2014	2013
Intragovernmental		
Accrued FECA Liability	$ 1,603	$ 1,689
Total Intragovernmental	1,603	1,689
Public		
Actuarial FECA Liability	7,167	7,233
Accrued Annual and Compensatory Leave	16,442	16,864
Contingent Liabilities	9,760	6,288
Foreign Service National After-Employment Benefits	8,554	4,444
Environmental and Disposal Liabilities	1,079	1,061
Total Liabilities Not Covered by Budgetary Resources	44,605	37,579
Total Liabilities Covered by Budgetary Resources	38,146	36,901
Total Liabilities	**$ 82,751**	**$ 74,480**

NOTE 9: FOREIGN SERVICE NATIONALS (FSN) AFTER-EMPLOYMENT BENEFITS

The BBG operates overseas in 24 countries and employs approximately 300 local nationals known as Foreign Service Nationals (FSNs). FSNs do not qualify for any federal civilian benefits, and therefore cannot participate in any of the federal civilian retirement plans. Instead, FSN employees participate in a variety of plans established by the Department of State in each country based upon prevailing wage and compensation practices in the host country, unless the Department of State makes a public interest determination to do so otherwise. In general, the BBG follows host country (i.e., local) practices and conventions in compensating FSNs. The end result of this is that compensation for FSNs is often not in accordance with what would otherwise be offered or required by statute and regulations for federal civilian employees.

In each country, FSN after-employment benefits are included in the Post's Local Compensation Plan (LCP). The LCP may include defined benefit plans, defined contribution plans, and retirement and voluntary severance lump sum payment plans. These plans are typically in addition to or in lieu of participating in the host country's local social security system. These benefits form an important part of the BBG's total compensation and benefits program that is designed to attract and retain highly skilled and talented FSN employees.

Local Defined Contribution Plans

The BBG has implemented various local arrangements with third party providers for defined contribution plans for the benefit of FSNs. Total contribution to these plans by the BBG in FY 2014 and FY 2013 were $81 thousand and $64 thousand, respectively.

Defined Benefit Plans

The BBG has implemented various arrangements for defined benefit pension plans for the benefit of FSNs in 4 countries. Some of these plans supplement the host country's equivalent to U.S. social security, others do not. While none of these supplemental plans are mandated by the host country, some are substitutes for optional tiers of a host country's social security system. Such arrangements include (but are not limited to) conventional defined benefit plans with assets held in the name of trustees of the plan who engage plan administrators, investment advisors and actuaries, and plans offered by insurance companies at predetermined rates or with annual adjustments to premiums. The BBG deposits funds under various fiduciary-type arrangements, purchases annuities under group insurance contracts or provides reserves to these plans. Benefits under the defined benefit plans are typically based either on years of service and/or the employee's compensation (generally during a fixed number of years immediately before retirement). The range of assumptions that are used for the defined benefit plans reflects the different economic and regulatory environments within the various countries.

The net defined benefit liability is comprised of the present value of the defined benefit obligation less the fair value of plan assets. The increase in our FY 2014 defined benefit plan liabilities is mostly attributable to FSN employees in Germany. In FY 2013, the BBG's liability relating to the German plan was based on an allocation of plan's total liabilities using the ratio of BBG employees compared to the presence of other Federal agencies. In FY 2014, the plan's actuary performed agency-specific actuarial valuations. This resulted in a more precise, increased actuarial liability estimate. The change in liability was an increase of $3,465 thousand in FY 2014.

Retirement and Voluntary Severance Lump Sum Payments

In 11 countries, FSN employees are provided a lump-sum separation payment when they resign, retire, or otherwise separate through no fault of their own. The amount of the payment is generally based on length of service, rate of pay at the time of separation, and the type of separation.

The cost method used for the valuation of the liabilities associated with these plans is the Projected Unit Credit actuarial cost method. The participant's benefit is first determined using both their projected service and salary at the retirement date. The projected benefit is then multiplied by the ratio of current service to projected service at retirement in order to determine an allocated benefit. The Projected Benefit Obligation (PBO) for the entire plan is calculated as the sum of the individual PBO amounts for each active member. Further, this calculation requires certain actuarial assumptions be made, such as voluntary withdraws, assumed retirement age, death and disability, as well as economic assumptions. These are done by the Department of State and its actuaries whose results are provided to the federal agencies for their use. The BBG relies on the actuarial reports to obtain required financial information.

The economic assumptions used for the Retirement and Voluntary Severance Lump Sum Payment Liability as of September 30, 2014 and 2013 are:

Economic Assumptions	2014	2013
Discount Rate	3.68%	3.66%
Rate of Inflation	2.31%	2.43%
Salary Increase	3.43%	3.55%

The total liabilities reported for the FSN After-employment Benefits as of September 30, 2014 and 2013, respectively, are as follows:

After-Employment Benefit Liability (in thousands)	2014	2013
Defined Benefits Plans	$ 4,385	$ 920
Voluntary Severance	2,012	1,439
Supplemental Retirement Lump Sum	2,157	2,085
Total After-Employment Benefit Liability	$ 8,554	$ 4,444

NOTE 10: ENVIRONMENTAL AND DISPOSAL LIABILITIES

Environmental and disposal liabilities result from hazardous and potentially hazardous materials at current operating locations and abandoned facilities that create a public health or environmental risk. The related cleanup cost to remove, contain or dispose of any hazardous materials or properties is recognized as an environmental and disposal liability until the end of the useful life of the PP&E or until the operations at the PP&E locations cease either permanently, temporarily, or until a voluntary remediation approach is adopted.

Federal, state, and local statutes and regulations require environmental cleanup. Some of these statutes include the Comprehensive Environmental Response, Compensation, and Liability Act; The Resource Conservation and Recovery Act; as well as State and Local laws.

The BBG recognizes an estimated $215 thousand in cleanup cost to remove hazardous materials from a transmitter facility. The estimate is based on recent disposal efforts.

Through an internal survey to comply with SFFAS 5, *Accounting for Liabilities of the Federal Government*, SFFAS 6, *Accounting for Property, Plant and Equipment*, FASAB Technical Bulletin 2006-1, *Recognition and Measurement of Asbestos-related Cleanup Costs* and Federal Financial Accounting and Auditing (FFAA) Technical Release 2, *Determining Probable and Reasonably Estimable for Environmental Liabilities in the Federal Government*, the BBG identified offices and building facilities that contained non-friable and friable asbestos. Based on this survey, the BBG recognized an estimated asbestos cleanup liability in the amount of $864 thousand in FY 2013 for four of its overseas facilities. This estimate was based on vendor quotes provided for asbestos clean-up efforts. The total environmental liability for BBG in FY 2014 is $1,079 thousands.

NOTE 11: OTHER LIABILITIES

Other liabilities consist of the following as of September 30, 2014 and 2013:

Other Liabilities (in thousands)	2014	2013
Intragovernmental		
Advances and Prepayments	$ 2,144	$ 1,381
Public		
Deposit and Suspense Liabilities	69	1,170
Total Other Liabilities	$ 2,213	$ 2,551

NOTE 12: OPERATING LEASE LIABILITY

The BBG leases real property in overseas and domestic locations under operating leases that expire in various years. The threshold for operating lease review and disclosure is $50,000. Minimum future lease payments under noncancellable operating leases having remaining terms in excess of one year as of September 30, 2014 for each of the next 5 years and in aggregate follows:

Operating Leases *(in thousands)*

Fiscal Year	Total
2015	$ 24,491
2016	22,853
2017	22,227
2018	21,835
2019	2,605
2020 and there after	1,903
Total Future Lease Payments	$ **95,914**

NOTE 13: CONTINGENT LIABILITIES

The BBG is a party in various administrative proceedings, legal actions, and tort claims that may ultimately result in settlements or decisions adverse to the Federal Government. These include legal cases that have been settled but not yet paid, and claims where the amount of potential loss is probable and estimable. The accrued amount related to a claim deemed probable in prior years received a court judgment in fiscal year 2014. It was determined this amount is to be paid via the Judgment Fund. The amount related to this claim was removed from the financial statements in accordance with Interpretation No. 2, *Accounting for Treasury Judgment Fund Transactions*, which is an interpretation of SFFAS #4 and #5. No amounts have been accrued in the financial records for claims where the amount of potential loss cannot be estimated or the likelihood of an unfavorable outcome is less than probable. The accrued and potential contingent liabilities as of September 30, 2014 and 2013 are as follows:

Contingent Liabilities *(in thousands)*

			Estimated Range of Loss	
FY 2014		Accrued Liabilities	Lower End of Range	Upper End of Range
Probable		$ 9,760	$ 9,760	$ 9,760
Reasonably Possible		-	-	225

			Estimated Range of Loss	
FY 2013		Accrued Liabilities	Lower End of Range	Upper End of Range
Probable		$ 6,288	$ 6,288	$ 6,288
Reasonably Possible		-	-	27,605

NOTE 14: INTRAGOVERNMENTAL COSTS AND EXCHANGE REVENUE

The following table presents the BBG's earned revenues and associated costs for providing goods and services to federal agencies and the public. Both earned revenues and related costs are allocated across the programs based on factors such as broadcasting hours and transmitting hours. Costs and exchange revenue for the years ended September 30, 2014 and 2013 consist of the following:

Programs (in thousands)	2014	2013
Voice of America (VOA)		
Intragovernmental Costs	$ 44,601	$ 53,307
Public Costs	304,048	317,268
Total VOA Costs	$ 348,649	$ 370,575
Intragovernmental Earned Revenues	$ (3,010)	$ (3,220)
Public Earned Revenues	(416)	(426)
Total VOA Earned Revenues	$ (3,426)	$ (3,646)
Office of Cuba Broadcasting (OCB)		
Intragovernmental Costs	$ 3,903	$ 5,233
Public Costs	45,532	40,537
Total OCB Costs	$ 49,435	$ 45,770
Surrogate Broadcasters		
Intragovernmental Costs	$ 3,594	$ 3,954
Public Costs	327,153	323,056
Total Surrogate Broadcasters Costs	$ 330,747	$ 327,010
Total Intragovernmental Costs	$ 52,098	$ 62,494
Total Public Costs	676,733	680,861
Total Intragovernmental Earned Revenue	(3,010)	(3,220)
Total Public Earned Revenue	(416)	(426)
Net Cost of Operations	$ 725,405	$ 739,709

NOTE 15: APPORTIONMENT CATEGORIES OF OBLIGATIONS INCURRED - DIRECT VS. REIMBURSABLE OBLIGATIONS

The BBG incurs obligations directly in support of its own programs as well as reimbursable obligations in support of other federal agencies' program initiatives. The reimbursable obligations incurred by the BBG support programs of the U.S. Agency for International Development and the Department of State.

Direct and reimbursable obligations for the years ended September 30, 2014 and 2013 are as follows:

Obligation Incurred (in thousands)	2014	2013
Direct Obligations Incurred		
CAT A	$ 524,970	$ 473,681
CAT B	205,398	245,003
Total Direct Obligations Incurred	**730,368**	**718,684**
Reimbursable Obligations Incurred		
CAT A	-	60
CAT B	3,959	5,286
Total Reimbursable Obligations Incurred	**$ 3,959**	**$ 5,346**

NOTE 16: UNDELIVERED ORDERS AT THE END OF THE PERIOD

Budgetary resources obligated for undelivered orders for the years ended September 30, 2014 and 2013 are $154.5 million and $134.3 million, respectively.

NOTE 17: EXPLANATION OF DIFFERENCES BETWEEN THE SBR AND THE BUDGET OF THE US GOVERNMENT

A comparison between the FY 2014 Statement of Budgetary Resources and the FY 2014 actual numbers presented in the FY 2016 Budget cannot be performed as the FY 2016 Budget is not yet available. The FY 2016 Budget is expected to be published in February 2015 and will be available from the Government Printing Office.

The BBG reconciled the amounts of the FY 2013 column on the statement of Budgetary Resources (SBR) to the actual amounts for FY 2013 in the 2014 President's Budget for budgetary resources, obligations incurred, distributed offsetting receipts and net outlays as presented below.

For the Fiscal Year Ended September 30, 2013 (in thousands)	Budgetary Resources	Obligations Incurred	Distributed Offsetting Receipts	Net Outlays
Combined Statement of Budgetary Resources	$ 770,806	$ 724,030	$ -	$ 711,473
Expired account	14,366	-	-	-
Undelivered Orders	16,012	-	-	-
Budget of the United States Government	**$ 740,428**	**$ 724,030**	**$ -**	**$ 711,473**

NOTE 18: RECONCILIATION OF NET COST OF OPERATIONS TO BUDGET

There are inherent differences in timing and recognition between the accrual proprietary accounting method used to calculate net cost and the budgetary accounting method used to report budgetary resources and obligations. The reconciliation of net cost to budgetary resources as of September 30, 2014 and 2013 is as follows:

Broadcasting Board of Governors
Reconciliation of Net Cost of Operations to Budget
For the Years Ended September 30, 2014 and 2013
(In Thousands)

	FY 2014	FY 2013
Resources Used to Finance Activities:		
Budgetary Resources Obligated		
Obligations incurred	734,327	724,030
Less: Spending Authority from Offsetting Collections and Recoveries	15,696	15,164
Obligations Net of Offsetting Collections and Recoveries	718,631	708,866
Less: Offsetting Receipts	-	-
Net Obligations	718,631	708,866
Other Resources		
Donations and Forfeitures of Property	-	1
Transfers in/out Without Reimbursement	1,220	-
Imputed Financing from costs Absorbed by Others	14,791	19,063
Other	(14)	(22)
Net Other Resources Used to Finance Activities	15,997	19,042
Total Resources Used to Finance Activities	**734,628**	**727,908**
Resources Used to Finance Items not Part of the Net Cost of Operations:		
Change in Budgetary Resources Obligated for Goods, Services and Benefits Ordered but Not Yet Provided	17,794	(20,525)
Resources that Fund Expenses Recognized in Prior Periods	574	6,696
Budgetary Offsetting Collections and Receipts That do not Affect Net Cost of Operations	-	-
Resources That Finance the Acquisition of Assets	2,176	7,512
Other Resources or Adjustments to Net Obligated Resources That do not Affect Net Cost of Operations	53	35
Total Resources Used to Finance Items not Part of the Net Cost of Operations	**20,597**	**(6,282)**
Total Resources Used to Finance the Net Cost of Operations	**714,031**	**734,190**

(Continues on next page)

Broadcasting Board of Governors
Reconciliation of Net Cost of Operations to Budget
For the Years Ended September 30, 2014 and 2013
(In Thousands) (Continued)

	FY 2014	FY 2013
Components of Net cost of Operations That Will not Require		
or Generate Resources in the Current Period:		
Components Requiring or Generating Resources in Future Periods:		
Increase in Annual Leave Liability	-	1,426
Increase in Environmental and Disposal Liability	18	1,061
Increase in Exchange Revenue Receivable From the Public	195	-
Other	7,636	252
Total Components of Net cost of Operations Requiring or		
Generating Resources in Future Periods	7,849	2,739
Components not Requiring or Generating Resources:		
Depreciation and Amortization	12,354	13,029
Revaluation of Assets or Liabilities	(9)	1,864
Other	(8,820)	(12,113)
Total Components of Net Cost of Operations not Requiring or Generating Resources	3,525	2,780
Total components of Net Cost of Operations That Will not Require or Generate		
Resources in the Current Period	11,374	5,519
Net Cost of Operations	$ 725,405	$ 739,709

The accompanying notes are an integral part of these statements.

Required Supplementary Information

Deferred Maintenance

Deferred maintenance is maintenance that was not performed when it should have been, that was scheduled and not performed, or that was delayed for a future period. Maintenance is the act of keeping property, plant, and equipment (PP&E) in acceptable operating condition and includes preventive maintenance, normal repairs, replacement of parts and structural components, and other activities needed to preserve the asset so that it can deliver acceptable performance and achieve its expected life. Maintenance excludes activities aimed at expanding the capacity of an asset or otherwise upgrading it to serve needs different from or significantly greater than those needs originally intended to be met by the asset.

The BBG has an ongoing maintenance and repair plan for its PP&E that allows it to prioritize required maintenance on its capitalized assets and schedule that maintenance appropriately. The maintenance plan is developed and updated by an inspection of its capital assets to determine current conditions and to estimate costs to correct any deficiencies. The inspection allows the BBG to assign a current condition code to each maintenance project. The five-point scale used for classifying the current condition of any asset requiring maintenance or repair is: 1 – excellent, 2 – good, 3 – fair, 4 – poor and 5 – very poor.

The BBG reviewed its FY 2014 maintenance and repair plan and identified those projects where maintenance or repair had been planned and/or required but nevertheless was not performed in 2014. For those projects where maintenance was not performed and where the current condition level was 4 or 5 (poor or very poor), the BBG estimated the deferred maintenance cost – the cost to return the asset to an acceptable condition.

The following shows BBG's deferred maintenance for projects for capital assets in condition code 4 – poor and condition code 5 – very poor that have been deferred as of September 30, 2014 and 2013:

Deferred Maintenance (in thousands)			
PP&E Category	Asset Condition	FY 2014 Estimated Cost to Return to Acceptable Condition	FY 2013 Estimated Cost to Return to Acceptable Condition
Equipment	4 - Poor	$ 250	$ -
	5 - Very Poor	18	-
	4 - Poor	536	280
Other Structures & Facilities	5 - Very Poor	50	-
Total		$ 854	$ 280

Section 4:
Other Information

Inspector General's Statement on FY 2014
Management and Performance Challenges 128

Agency Response to the Management
and Performance Challenges 131

Summary of Financial Statement Audit
and Management Assurances 134

Reporting on Improper Payments Information Act 136

Inspector General's Statement on Management and Performance Challenges

INSPECTOR GENERAL'S ASSESSMENT OF MANAGEMENT AND PERFORMANCE CHALLENGES – BROADCASTING BOARD OF GOVERNORS

The *eports Consolidation Act of 2000* requires that the *Performance and Accountability Report* of the Broadcasting Board of Governors (BBG) include a statement by the Inspector General that summarizes the most serious management and performance challenges facing BBG and briefly assesses the progress in addressing them. The Office of Inspector General (OIG) considers the most serious management and performance challenges for BBG to be in the following areas:

1. Establishing a Chief Executive Officer
2. Managing Contracts, Acquisitions, and Grants
3. Broadcasting with Fewer Resources
4. Financial and Property Management
   . Information Security and Management

1. Establishing a Chief Executiv Officer

Implementing a management structure that provides effective oversight to all broadcasting operations at BBG remains a challenge. BBG still does not have a Chief Executive Officer (CEO) to coordinate all operational aspects of U.S. international broadcasting. In the 2013 inspection of BBG,[1] OIG found that a part-time board could not provide effective oversight to all broadcasting operations. OIG recommended that BBG establish a CEO position, a topic that was also outlined in BBG's 2012–2016 strategic plan.

To mitigate this management challenge, in January 2014, BBG established an interim management structure for its International Broadcasting Bureau and appointed three senior executives to manage day-to-day operations: a Director of Global Operations, a Director of Global Strategy, and a Director of Global Communications. Until a CEO is hired, these Global Directors provide oversight and direction to the Directors of Voice of America, the Office of Cuba Broadcasting (OCB), and the other offices. On September 23, 2014, BBG announced that it had identified whom it intends to hire as CEO.[2]

2. Managing Contracts, Acquisitions, and Grants

In the inspection report of OCB, OIG reported several weaknesses in contract administration procedures and oversight.[3] This is an ongoing management challenge. OIG found that BBG's Office of Contracts was not appointing, in writing, contracting officer's representatives for OCB contracts, although this is required by the Federal Acquisition Regulation.

OIG also audited BBG's acquisition functions to evaluate whether BBG had adequate acquisition policies and procedures.[4] Based on a review of 34 contracts, totaling $7.8 million, OIG identified noncompliance with Federal contracting regulations, a lack of contract oversight, and violations of the Antideficiency Act (ADA). Specifically, OIG determined that BBG had routinely entered into personal services contracts that exceeded its statutory authority. This is a violation of the ADA, which prohibits "employ[ing] personal services exceeding that authorized by law." BBG also obligated funds before the funds were available by allowing contractors to work without contracts in place via a "pre-approval" process, which resulted in two reportable violations of the ADA. Further, BBG did not comply with Federal regulations for conducting selected acquisition functions, including contract oversight, in support of the BBG mission. As a result, BBG did not have reasonable assurance that its needs were

---

[1] *Inspection of the Broadcasting Board of Governors* (ISP-IB-13-07, January 2013).
[2] www.bbg.gov/blog/2014/09/23/bbg-names-andy-lack-ceo/.
[3] *Inspection of the Office of Cuba Broadcasting* (ISP-IB-14-15, July 2014).
[4] *Audit of the Broadcasting Board of Governors Administration and Oversight of Acquisition Functions* (AUD CG IB-14-26, June 2014).

1

met in the most effective, economical, and timely manner. o
The audit report identified the following:R

- R more than $400,000 in funds that, because of noncom-o
  pliance, could be put to better use relating to contracts o
  that were never executed;o
- R about $24,000 in questioned costs attributable to a lack R
  f contract oversight; and o
- R more than $475,000 in unauthorized commitments. R

Finally, the audit report identified a systemic failure of BBG's R
acquisition function, indicating that BBG is at risk for fraud, o
waste, and abuse in acquisitions, as well as for potential o
conflicts of interest.R

BBG funds three grantees through annual grant agree-o
ments: Radio Free Europe/Radio Liberty (RFE/RL), Radio R
Free Asia, and Middle East Broadcasting Networks (MBN). R
OIG reported that BBG did not have sufficient oversight of R
these grantees. In one report,[5] OIG noted that BBG did not o
have procedures in place for post-award grantee moni-o
toring to ensure that Federal awards were used only for o
allowable costs. OIG also reported that BBG did not have o
sufficient oversight policies and procedures to ensure that R
grantees have mandated procurement procedures. Further, o
BBG did not record significant cash balances provided to R
grantees in its annual financial statements. R

In another audit report,[6] OIG noted that BBG did not suf-o
ficiently monitor one grantee, did not adequately define R
grantee oversight roles and responsibilities, and did not o
maintain adequate internal communications pertaining to o
grantee oversight. According to BBG, it is placing a high o
priority on addressing the weakness in grants monitoring o
identified by the financial statement audits. In FY 2014, BBG R
developed a Corrective Action Plan that outlined certain o
control improvements for grantee monitoring. As of August o
2014, this plan had not been substantively implemented. R

3. Broadcasting With Fewer Resources

BBG continues to have problems properly aligning o
resources with its technologies, targeted countries, and o
broadcasting activities.[7] In its FY 2014 budget request, BBG R
proposed merging RFE/RL's Radio Free Iraq with MBN, at R
an estimated savings of $1.7 million.oSimilarly, in its last R

three budget requests, BBG proposed closing the Poro o
transmission facility in the Philippines for an estimated o
savings of approximately $300,000. No transmissions are o
originating from the Poro transmitting station; BBG stated o
that all needed transmissions in FY 2015 can be accom-o
modated at other facilities.[9R]

BBG has also taken steps to reduce its operating expenses. o
In the United Arab Emirates, MBN and RFE/RL journalists R
share studio space. The journalist from RFE/RL also reports R
to Voice of America's Persian News Network. R

4. Financial and Property Management

Financial management continues to be a challenge for o
BBG. In FY 2013, BBG received an unqualified opinion R
on its financial statements.R Although this is a positive o
achievement, the independent auditor identified R
significant internal control deficiencies related to R
financial management, as well as significant instances R
f noncompliance with laws and regulations that were o
significant to the financial statement audit. For example, R
the audit found that BBG had materially misstated o
its assets and expenses because it did not record o
90 transmitting stations as assets. Further, BBG had not R
recorded improvements to leases as required and did not o
properly account for leases. o

To address this deficiency, BBG's financial team has R
been working closely with the property team to develop o
comprehensive policies and procedures to account o
for property-related items. BBG management has also o
implemented additional controls over the identification R
f capitalized assets, including assessing all contracts over o
the capitalization threshold; in the past, only expenditures o
were being examined. In addition, management o
has enhanced their processes and communication o
methodologies for accumulating lease information. o

The audit also found that BBG lacked sufficient, reliable R
controls over its accounting and business processes o
to ensure that budgetary transactions were properly o
recorded, monitored, and reported. In FY 2014, R
BBG designated this area as a high priority, and the o
Office of Contracts is working to implement concise R
methodologies on how to properly record and monitor o

---

[5] RAudit of the Broadcasting Board of Governors FY 2013 Financial Statements (AUD-FM-IB-14-14, December 2013).R

[6] RAudit of Radio Free Europe/Radio Liberty After-employment Benefits (AUD-FM-IB-14-34, September 2014).R

[7] RInspection of Embassy Abu Dhabi and Consulate General Dubai, United Arab Emirates (ISP-I-14-11A, May 2014).R

[8] RBroadcasting Board of Governors FY 2014 Budget Request.R

[9] RBroadcasting Board of Governors FY 2013, FY 2014, and FY 2015 Budget Request documents.R

[10] Audit of the Broadcasting Board of Governors FY 2013 Financial Statements (AUD-FM-IB-14-14, December 2013).R

procurement transactions to ensure that they will be more s accurately reported. The audit also found that BBG did not s have a process in place to annually evaluate and report on the s ef ectiveness of its internal control and financial management systems that protect the integrity of Federal programs as s required by the Federal Managers' Financial Integrity Act. s BBG management has indicated that BBG plans to implement s a robust internal control program in FY 2015 and FY 2016 f that will address known weaknes es related to documenting, s testing, and asses ing internal control over operations and s internal control over financial reporting.f

In the inspection of the OCB, OIG identified weaknesses f related to property management and unliquidated obli-s gations monitoring.[11] OIG found a lack of compliance in s property management procedures for all nonexpendable s and sensitive property, capitalized property inventory, and s inventory and disposal procedures. Although BBG has a pro-s ces in place to review unliquidated obligations, OIG found s that OCB was not reviewing its unliquidated balances for s potential de-obligation.s

5. Information and Security Management

During the FY 2014 audit of BBG's compliance with f the Federal Information Security Management Act f (FISMA) of 2002, OIG found that weaknesses noted from the FY 2013 report continued to exist and several components of BBG's information security s management program have not been completed. s Since FY 2013, BBG has taken steps to improve its f information security program. Although BBG's efforts s have resulted in some improvements, collectively, s the information security control weaknesses that s OIG identified in this audit represent a significant f deficiency to enterprise-wide security. OIG f determined that BBG had not effectively developed s and managed the risk management framework, s continuous monitoring program, system-specific f and enterprise-wide contingency plans, configuration f management, and the incident response and s reporting program. Other information security s program areas that need improvement are plans of s action and milestones, remote access, identity and s acces management, and security training. s

---

[11] s*Inspection of the Office of Cuba Broadcasting* (ISP-IB-14-15, July 2014).f

Agency Response to the Management and Performance Challenges

The BBG has reviewed the OIG report identifying findings regarding the most serious management and performance challenges facing the Broadcasting Board of Governors (BBG). The BBG has reviewed the OIG findings and would like to take this opportunity to describe the actions that it is taking to address the management and performance challenges identified by the OIG

ESTABLISHING A CHIEF EXECUTIVE OFFICER

The BBG concurs with the recommendation to establish a Chief Executive Officer (CEO) for the Agency.

After an aggressive search effort, the Board has chosen Andrew Lack to be the CEO of U.S. International Media. Having served as former Chairman and CEO of Media Group at Bloomberg L.P., Chairman and CEO of Sony Music Entertainment, and other senior positions in U.S. commercial news and media companies, Mr. Lack will ensure that the BBG can most effectively address the rapidly evolving global media environment and begin to address the BBG's ongoing strategic challenges and needed operational reforms. Mr. Lack is anticipated to start in the first quarter of FY 2015.

MANAGING CONTRACTS, ACQUISITIONS, AND GRANTS

The BBG acknowledges weaknesses in its contract administration procedures and oversight, its acquisition policies and procedures, and grantee oversight. The BBG continues to work with OIG on closing the recommendations resulting from OIG's audit of the Agency's acquisition function. In response to the recommendations, management has issued Agency-wide guidance regarding certain Federal Acquisition Regulation compliance issues, has retained expert consultants to assist in the implementation of acquisition improvements, and is working to update specific policies and procedures in its Broadcasting Administrative Manual, the authoritative compilation of policies that affect BBG's operations. In addition, the Agency has made progress toward its goal of obtaining the assistance of certain contractors through one or more staffing agencies to address risks identified by OIG related to the procurement of personal services.

In response to OIG concerns about grantee oversight, the Agency has taken steps to strengthen its oversight of grant awards, beginning with a full review of its current grant monitoring program. BBG has obtained the assistance of KPMG to aid in this review, which should promote the development of a more robust monitoring program.

BROADCASTING WITH FEWER RESOURCES

As noted by the OIG, the BBG has worked, and continues to work, to reduce its operating expenses and better manage and align its resources in this tight fiscal environment. In addition to reducing its operating expenses in the UAE by sharing resources between networks, the BBG has initiated an intensive effort to harmonize operations in several other key markets. Significant progress has been made in broadcasts to Iran and the Caucasus.

As a result of harmonization efforts in Iran, BBG has created a single satellite television stream, managed by VOA and including RFE/RL content; a single audio stream, managed by RFE/RL and distributed via shortwave and medium wave, satellite audio, and Web streaming; and a single, joint digital stream, managed by RFE/RL. RFE/RL is scaling up video production for the joint television stream, and VOA is providing Washington reports for RFE/RL's audio programming. VOA is shifting its website to focus on its television programs and personalities, and will link to RFE/RL's full-service news site.

In the Caucasus, RFE/RL Armenian is reducing radio output and relying on VOA to serve as its Washington Bureau. VOA will focus primarily on television, and RFE/RL will run a joint website featuring content from both brands. In Azerbaijani, RFE/RL is taking the lead on a satellite television channel to which VOA is contributing daily newscasts and a magazine program. VOA is ending its radio programming, and RFE/RL is scaling back radio in favor of satellite television, by far the more popular platform. And, in Georgia, both networks are contributing audio content to a joint 18-hour-per-day audio stream on a nationwide FM network, led by RFE/RL. RFE/RL also is taking the lead on a joint website, which features content from both brands.

In addition, the BBG is looking to reduce costs using technology. As part of a major effort to reduce telecommunications costs and move toward a more flexible and advanced global delivery data network, the BBG completed the first phase of the Agency migration from expensive, dedicated transoceanic satellite and fiber circuits to more flexible and less expensive digital Multi-Protocol Label Switching (MPLS) circuits. In FY 2014, BBG connected two major BBG distribution hubs in the Philippines and Germany to the Agency's global MPLS network.

The BBG is also reducing its operating expenses by consolidating and modernizing its workspace in its Wilbur J. Cohen Building headquarters. The BBG is transforming 35,000 square feet of space from private offices to a more modern, open workspace. This ongoing initiative (BBG has identified an additional 50,000 square feet of office to convert to an open design) will help the BBG save money by accommodating higher staffing levels while leasing less office space.

FINANCIAL AND PROPERTY MANAGEMENT

As expressed in the OIG findings, the BBG is continuing ongoing efforts to improve financial management within the challenge of constrained staffing and resources. The BBG will continue to focus efforts to improve controls and strengthen the processes for financial management, financial audits, budgetary transactions, procurement transactions, and internal control systems. The BBG will also work closely with OCB and other federal elements to ensure compliance with current processes to efficiently track and resolve outstanding unliquidated obligations.

INFORMATION AND SECURITY MANAGEMENT

The BBG appreciates the OIG's identification of areas for improvement in information technology and security. The Agency will continue to take steps to improve its information technology and security program.

The BBG will work to complete all the required annual FISMA security reassessments during FY 2015 as the Agency adopts the Risk Management Framework in the National Institute of Standards and Technology (NIST). The Agency will ensure that continuous monitoring programs demonstrate progress towards a robust implementation of all NIST standards. The BBG is addressing weaknesses in security configurations of remote computers by developing a continuous monitoring program to ensure that authorization and access control is consistently enforced. In addition, the BBG has accelerated issuance of personal Identity Verification cards to its employees and contractors, and the CIO will take steps to develop and implement a role-based IT security training program in accordance with guidance from the NIST.

Summary of Financial Statement Audit and Management Assurances

TABLE 1

Summary of Financial Statement Audit

Audit Opinion	Unmodified				
Restatement	No				
Material Weaknesses	Beginning Balance	New	Resolved	Consolidated	Ending Balance
Grantee Monitoring & Advance	1				1
Property, Plant, and Equipment	1				1
Budgetary Accounting and Funds Control	1				1
Total Material Weaknesses	3				3

TABLE 2

Summary of Management Assurances

Effectiveness of Internal Control over Financial Reporting (FMFIA § 2)						
Statement of Assurance	Statement of No Assurance					
Material Weaknesses	Beginning Balance	New	Resolved	Consolidated	Reassessed	Ending Balance
Total Material Weaknesses	*N/A*					
Effectiveness of Internal Control over Operations (FMFIA § 2)						
Statement of Assurance	Statement of No Assurance					
Material Weaknesses	Beginning Balance	New	Resolved	Consolidated	Reassessed	Ending Balance
Total Material Weaknesses	*N/A*					
Conformance with financial management system requirements (FMFIA § 4)						
Statement of Assurance	Statement of No Assurance					
Non-Conformances	Beginning Balance	New	Resolved	Consolidated	Reassessed	Ending Balance
Total Non-Conformances						

Reporting on Improper Payment Information Act, as Amended by IPERIA

Improper payments are payments that should not have been made or were made in the incorrect amount, which can include duplicate payments, payments to ineligible receipients, or payments made without sufficient supporting documentation. To improve the integrity and accuracy of the federal Government's payments, Congress enacted the *Improper Payments Information Act (IPIA) of 2002 (P.L. 107-300)*. IPIA requires federal agencies to:

- Review their programs and activities annually;
- Identify programs that may be susceptible to significant improper payments;
- Estimate amounts improperly paid; and
- Report improper payment amounts and the actions taken to reduce them.

During July 2010, Congress passed the *Improper Payments Elimination and Recovery Act (IPERA)* which amended IPIA and Section 831 of the *Defense Authorization Act of 2002*, also known as the Recovery Auditing Act. IPERA strengthened IPIA by increasing management accountability and requiring additional efforts to recover improper payments.

In January 2013, Congress enacted the *Improper Payments Elimination and Recovery Improvement Act of 2012*, (IPERIA) "to intensify efforts to identify, prevent, and recover payment error, waste, fraud".[1] It reinforces and accelerates the "Do Not Pay" initiative, increases emphasis on high-priority programs, establishes performance targets, and clarifies guidance for estimating improper payments.

OMB Memorandum M-15-02 dated October 20, 2014 provides the latest guidance to agencies for implementing IPIA, IPERA, and IPERIA. This guidance is contained in Parts I and II of Appendix C to *OMB Circular A-123, Management's Responsibility for Internal Controls* which requires all executive branch agencies to determine whether the risk of improper payments is significant (exceeds both 1.5 percent of program annual payments and $10 million, or exceeds $100 million annually) and to provide valid annual estimates of improper payments for programs or activities that are susceptible to significant improper payments.

---

[1] Public Law 112-248

BBG'S PROCESS

The BBG is dedicated to continuing to strengthen its improper payments program to ensure payments are legitimate, processed correctly and efficiently. The Program utilizes an experienced and trained staff, a financial management system that is designed with control functions to mitigate risk, and an internal analysis of processes and transactions. All executives and staff are required to comply with BBG's procurement and accounting policies and procedures, and Federal laws and regulations.

The BBG conducts the following steps to comply with the IPIA, IPERA, and IPERIA and OMB Circular A-123 Appendix C:

1. Reviews all programs and activities and identifies those that are susceptible to significant improper payments.

2. Obtains a statistically valid estimate of the annual amount of improper payments for those programs that are identified as susceptible to significant improper payments.

3. Implements a plan to reduce erroneous payments.

4. For those programs that are identified as susceptible to significant improper payments, reports estimates of the annual amount of improper payments in programs and activities and BBG's progress in reducing them.

The BBG's Office of Chief Financial Officer (OCFO) is responsible for reviewing and reporting the BBG's improper payments annually. The above four-step process began during fiscal year 2012 and continues into fiscal year 2015.

RISK ASSESSMENT

The BBG's qualitative risk assessment methodology consists of ranking each of its programs based on operational risk, complexity, volume of payments, human capital risk, historical risk, IT risk, compliance risk and total dollar value. For good governance, the BBG also conducts testing to estimate the improper payment rate of all programs on a rotational basis, currently testing each program once every three years.

For FY 2014, the BBG reviewed two programs, the Office of Technology, Services and Innovation (TSI) and Radio Free Asia (RFA), extracting the universe of payments from the BBG's financial system, Momentum, for the period of October 1, 2013 through September 30, 2014, excluding overseas payments, intra-governmental transactions and payroll. The BBG reviewed the full population of payments for RFA and a sample of 172 payments for TSI, which included all payments made for more than $1 million and a random selection for the remainder of the sample. No improper payments were identified in the RFA program. The TSI had an error rate of 7.16%, due to incomplete or insufficient documentation which prevented the BBG from verifying whether the payment was proper. When projected to the population this error rate resulted in an estimated $6 million gross improper payments, which is below OMB's threshold for programs at significant risk.

Based on the results of the BBG's qualitative and quantitative risk assessment, there were no programs which met OMB's criteria for being susceptible to significant improper payments (exceeding both 1.5 percent of program payments and $10 million).

RECAPTURE OF IMPROPER PAYMENT REPORTING

IPERA requires agencies to conduct payment recapture audits for each program and activity that expends $1 million or more annually, if conducting such audits would be cost-effective. A payment recapture audit is a detective and corrective control activity designed specifically to identify and recapture overpayments.

The BBG contracted with a CPA firm to provide recapture audit services on a contingency fee basis. Based on the results of the improper payment estimates, prior year recapture audit results (which found no improper payments), and the BBG's payment composition (large volume, low dollar payments), the contractor determined that it would not be cost-effective to further pursue a recapture audit. The BBG notified the OIG and the OMB a recapture audit would not be performed for FY 2014.

The BBG also identifies and recaptures improper payments during the normal course of its disbursement management process. During FY 2014, the BBG identified twenty-five erroneous payments, totaling $53,945. During FY 2013, the BBG identified twenty-five erroneous payments totaling $170,737. All but $13,345 of the amount identified in 2014 has been recovered. The 2014 amount outstanding has been transferred to the Treasury Offset Program for collection. The amounts identified and recovered are shown in Table 1.

Table 1:
Overpayments Recaptured Outside of Payment Recapture Audit (in thousands)

Source of Recovery		Self Reported
Program/Bureau		VOA, IBB, TSI
Type of Payment		Other
Amount Subject to Review for 2014 Reporting		N/A
2014 Actual Amount Reviewed and Reported		N/A
2014 Amount Identified for Recovery	$	54
2014 Amount Recovered	$	41
2014 % of Amount Recovered out of Amount Identified		76.00%
2014 Amount Outstanding	$	13
2014 % of Amount Outstanding out of Amount Identified		24.00%
2014 Amount Determined Not to be Collectable	$	0.00
2014 % of Amount Determined Not to be Collectable out of Amount Identified		0.00%
2013 Amount Identified for Recovery	$	171
2013 Amount Recovered	$	171

BBG INFORMATION SYSTEMS AND OTHER INFRASTRUCTURE

The BBG believes that it has sufficient internal controls, human capital, and information systems to detect and prevent improper payments. The BBG's vouchers are processed within the financial management system (Momentum) by well-trained examiners and certifying officers prior to submission to the Department of the Treasury. The financial accounting system, Momentum, has built in controls to prevent duplicate invoice processing, ensure the availability of funds, require payment authorizations, and enforce access controls. If an erroneous payment occurs the BBG takes immediate action to collect those funds.

The BBG's Improper Payment Program is functional and designed to prevent material, recurring, and illegitimate payments. The BBG standard operating procedure provides control processes to ensure that erroneous or fraudulent payments do not occur.

BARRIERS

The BBG has not identified any barriers which would limit its corrective actions in reducing improper payments.

AGENCY REDUCTION OF IMPROPER PAYMENTS WITH THE DO NOT PAY INITIATIVE

The Do Not Pay Initiative directs agencies to check various databases to identify ineligible recipients and prevent or detect fraud or errors. Currently the BBG submits a monthly batch file of vendors paid to the Do Not Pay databases to verify eligibility. In FY 2014, no payments were identified as improper due to these checks. On occasion, exceptions were initially identified and later determined to be eligible recipients upon further review. Table 2 provides the dollar amounts and the number of payments reviewed using the Death Master File (DMF) during the period October 1, 2013 through August 31, 2014. The DMF is produced by the Social Security Administration (SSA) and contains over 85 million death records reported to the SSA from 1936 to present.

Table 2:

Do Not Pay Initiative (in thousands)

Table 2: Implementation of the Do Not Pay Initiative to Prevent Improper Payments (in thousands)						
	Number (#) of Payments reviewed for improper payments	Dollars ($) of payments reviewed for improper payments	Number (#) of payments stopped	Dollars ($) of payments stopped	Number (#) of improper payments reviewed and not stopped	Dollars ($) of improper payments reviewed and not stopped
Reviews with the DMF only	15	$ 351,948	-	-	-	-

www.ingramcontent.com/pod-product-compliance
Lightning Source LLC
Chambersburg PA
CBHW080256290526
45790CB00005B/1828